PROGRESS AND SURVIVAL

EMILE BENOIT

PROGRESS AND SURVIVAL

An Essay on the Future of Mankind

edited by
Jack Benoit Gohn

PRAEGER

PRAEGER SPECIAL STUDIES • PRAEGER SCIENTIFIC

Library of Congress Cataloging in Publication Data

Benoit, Emile.
 Progress and survival.

 Includes bibliographical references and index.
 1. Progress. 2. Economic policy. 3. Social
policy. 4. Human ecology. 5. Civilization, Modern--
1950-   I. Gohn, Jack Benoit. II. Title.
HM101.B4718   303.4   80-14423
 ISBN 0-03-056911-7

Grateful acknowledgment is hereby made to the following for permission to use copyrighted material: "Full Employment Policy Revisited," by Emile Benoit. April 28, 1973 issue. Reprinted by permission of *The New Republic*, © 1973, The New Republic, Inc. "Must Growth Stop?" by Emile Benoit. Reprinted with permission from the May 1972 issue of the *Columbia Journal of World Business*. Copyright © 1972 by the Trustees of Columbia University in the City of New York. "What Future Spaceship Earth?" by Emile Benoit. December 1973 issue of *Social Policy*. Reprinted with permission of the Social Policy Corporation. "The Inflation-Unemployment Tradeoff and Full Economic Recovery," by Emile Benoit. October 1975 issue. Reprinted by permission of the *American Journal of Economics and Sociology*. "Development through Restraints on Material Growth," by Emile Benoit. Adapted from *Focus*, November-December 1974. Copyright © 1974 by the American Geographical Society of New York. Used by permission. "The Coming Age of Shortages," "A Dynamic Equilibrium Economy," and "First Steps to Survival," by Emile Benoit. January through March 1976. Reprinted by permission of the *Bulletin of the Atomic Scientists*, a magazine of science and public affairs. Copyright © 1976 by the Educational Foundation for Nuclear Science, Chicago, Illinois.

Published in 1980 by Praeger Publishers
CBS Educational and Professional Publishing
A Division of CBS, Inc.
521 Fifth Avenue, New York, New York 10017 U.S.A.

© 1980 by Praeger Publishers

0123456789   038   987654321

Printed in the United States of America

FOREWORD
Kenneth Boulding

E mile Benoit was a rare person in more than one sense. As an economist he was unusually competent; but more than that, he had a breadth of vision that was rare among economists. He saw economics always as a tool and a stepping stone to a larger appreciation of the complexities of the real world. As a friend he was a rare person, a delight to be with—sensitive, kindly, gentle, full of ideas, yet rigorous and disciplined. Nothing shoddy got by him. As a writer he was rare in that nothing that he did was overdone. His style is always clear but always retains a sense of something left unsaid. His work *Disarmament and the Economy*[1] was a pioneering book, which opened up a whole new subject—the interaction between the war industry and the economy and the rest of society. His later work on this subject *Defense and Eonomic Growth in Developing Countries*[2] combined two major interests of his life—development and the world economy and the role of the war industry in that development. Some of the results were not wholly to his liking, but his deep honesty and integrity made him publish what he found whether he liked it or not.

The present volume is a fitting "Amen" to his career as a writer. It reflects the deep convictions and anxieties of his later years. One cannot help but be moved by its intensity of concern for the human race and by the agony of the spectacle of it galloping like a lemming to its likely destruction. Nevertheless, this is not a pessimistic book. It is filled with a profound hope that we can respond to warnings, perceive cliffs ahead, and steer ourselves away from them. Benoit's book is a radar reflecting the dangers ahead and pointing out other paths by which they might be avoided. In detail, though not in spirit, it is inevitably an interim report, and in many details it is open to criticism. My own view is that the next 50 years may well be a little better than he portrays them, but this in no way diminishes neither the significance nor the urgency of coming to terms with the long-range problem of a sustainable society. This idea is not new, but I think I have never seen it put forward with such eloquence as in this volume. But his book is not mere eloquence; it is full of highly practical suggestions—for instance, on such rather technical matters as the unemployment-inflation issue.

The book has been put together with great skill by Emile Benoit's son, Jack Benoit Gohn, from manuscripts on which the author had been working at the time of his death. It is a beautiful tribute of a son to the memory of his father. But it is much more than a memorial; it carries a message that the world needs to hear. In practical ways it leads to hope rather than despair.

NOTES

1. Emile Benoit and Kenneth E. Boulding, eds., *Disarmament and the Economy* (New York: Harper & Row, 1963).
2. Emile Benoit, *Defense and Economic Growth in Developing Countries* (Lexington, Mass.: D. C. Heath, 1973).

PREFACE DEDICATORY
Emile Benoit

*To my great-great-grandchildren in 2076
and to the memory of Arthur O. Lovejoy*

I am beginning this book about the future of mankind in the United States's bicentennial year in the hope that copies of it will be delivered to my great-great-grandchildren 100 years from now. I realize that the odds are, unfortunately, against that happening, since what I am doing is like enclosing a message in a bottle and casting it into the sea. The vast void of time may be even harder to cross than the empty expanse of ocean. For not only must the message pass through time but through the medium of our society, which could disintegrate by then, for reasons discussed in this book. Yet I have not given up on the hope that this message *will* reach you, since—as I show in the book—the problems ahead are inherently soluble if we are sufficiently innovative and open-minded.

You may well by then regard me as a bit of ancient history. To be sure, I am much too old ever to meet you. But there may be two persons we both have known: Elizabeth and Andrew, my grandchildren, your grandparents. Thus, by my influence on them through my son and their influence on you through your parents, I may have some slight family influence on you. In any case you will inherit a few of my genes. And if you read this book—even if by then most of it is "old hat"—you may still be influenced in one way or another.

You, on your side, have influenced me—or at least the thought of you has. It is because I feared for what would happen to your generation, and later generations, that I wrote this book. As I show, our "growth" and "prosperity" up to now have been essentially a matter of robbing future generations of their birthright for *our* benefit. I have tried to develop an alternative set of policies that would enable the present generation to achieve rising standards of welfare *without* making life harder and more dangerous for future generations.

I am also dedicating this book to the memory of the philosopher Arthur O. Lovejoy. He was my chief mentor—and a member of my dissertation committee at Harvard—and had a greater intellectual impact on me than did any other person. I liked and admired as well as respected him—perhaps "stood in awe of him" would be more accurate. He had the most penetrating intellect accompanied by the most overwhelming erudition that I have ever encountered.

In dedicating this book to one who is dead and to others who are not yet living, I emphasize the crucial role of the links between the generations for the survival of our race. The motto of *après nous le déluge* is a sure recipe for racial suicide. Only if we revere what is good in the past and those who created it, and look upon ourselves as trustees, with the obligation to cherish, improve, and transmit it to future generations, will future generations continue to exist.

Now as to this book itself. It is a brief and plain survey of the chief problems threatening to destroy mankind. It goes on to outline a set of policies for solving these problems. Unlike certain other books, it tries to cover not just one or two key world problems but the whole wide range of world problems, exploring their interrelations. Necessarily, it gives primary emphasis to long-term rather than short-term problems and to basic rather than superficial ones. And it considers these problems not from the narrow viewpoint of a single discipline, like economics, but in a highly interdisciplinary way. I am convinced that unless one looks at our present institutions from the outside—with the insights provided by economics, sociology, anthropology, psychology, philosophy, political science, and international relations—one is bound to be mired in ethnocentric parochialism and to lack any imaginative vision of how our institutions might be fundamentally improved. Finally, the primary emphasis is not on the problems but on the solutions: the new policies required, how they could be implemented, and how the political resistances to them might be overcome.

It stands to reason that a book as short as this, covering such a wide and largely unknown terrain, cannot hope to be definitive. This is no more than a preliminary sketch, calling people's attention to upcoming problems and possible solutions. There will be plenty of time for improvements and more technical approaches by others. My job here is merely to make people aware of the problems and the fact that solutions exist. If I can succeed in doing that, then I shall have truly served as a link between the two generations represented by the dedicatees of this book.

I would like to express my thanks to the following persons who at one time or another have encouraged me to develop certain ideas featured in this book or to put these ideas into book form. They are: Professor Kenneth Boulding, Representative Morris Udall, Professor Harold C. Urey, Dr. Phillip Handler, Dr. Leonard Silk, Dr. Marshall Robinson, Professor John T. Edsall, Dr. Henry W. Kendall, Professor Preston Cloud, Dr. John H. G. Pierson, Dean George F. James, Dean Harvey Picker, Dean James W. Kuhn, Mrs. Etta Benoit, Professor Raymond Smullyan, and Dr. Jack Benoit Gohn.

I am also indebted to President William McGill of Columbia University and Deans Louis Volpp, James Heffernan, and Doris Yavitz, who helped provide the necessary facilities by recommending me for the title of Senior Research Associate. And I am particularly indebted to my secretary, Harriet Leonard, for extraordinarily conscientious and efficient help over many years, even when seriously overburdened.

CONTENTS

1
Why care?

Most men care about their own survival. A good many are willing to risk it to aid the survival of a particular nation, city-state, tribe, faction, et cetera. But, except to a few, illuminated by religion, idealism, or scientific reflection, mankind as a whole has appeared as too much of an abstraction to inspire much concern. Anyhow, there was no reason to suppose that it was endangered. Now that it *is* endangered, attitudes have hardly changed. Mankind, the only species capable of imagining its own extinction, seems unconcerned at the prospect—providing that prospect can only be deferred for a generation or two. The importance of human survival is disputed by few but ignored in practice by the majority.

FUNDAMENTAL ARGUMENTS

This lack of concern is sometimes justified by such flippancies as "What has posterity ever done for me?" or by pleadings that our immediate problems are too urgent and engrossing to give us the leisure and resources to deal with long-run problems. Some would have us continue to count on Divine Providence, or luck, or science—pointing out that we have always been able to pull through in the past. And some skeptics may even be willing to articulate the underlying doubts: If our descendants are wiped out, is that necessarily so tragic? Can they expect to live forever? And so long as we ourselves get by, does it really make much difference how much longer the human comedy is carried on? In this book I am primarily concerned with how to survive—not whether it is worth surviving. Nevertheless, it seemed worth starting off with at least a few words about why some of us value human survival and believe that many others will, too, once they realize that it is endangered.

A friend of mine once remarked that the death of an individual, leaving grieving family and friends behind, might be tragic but that the sudden wiping out of the *whole* human race at the same time, as in a nuclear holocaust, would not necessarily be such a bad thing. This raises the key issue very sharply. Was he really right?

Nevil Shute in an imaginative tour de force of a novel called *On The Beach* (1957) conveyed well a sense of the gnawing, though heavily alcoholized, anguish of the last remnant of mankind, in their final days, facing extinction from rising levels of radiation after an atomic war, as they poison themselves one by one when, or just before, the dreaded symptoms of acute radiation illness appear. Clearly, the ending of mankind would not necessarily be a neat and tidy affair. Indeed, some of the ways in which mankind may be destroyed could involve a long period of fear, disorganization, and general misery, worse in total than the whole history of human suffering up to that time. And extinction by pollution, by industrial breakdown from raw material shortages, or by slow starvation would not necessarily be any less awful to endure than death by nuclear radiation.

But even if death were mercifully sudden for everyone, this would not mitigate the essential tragedy of the ending of mankind, which goes much beyond the death of particular individuals—who, of course, have to die sooner or later anyhow. The crux of the tragedy would lie not in the death of the older generation, or even in the premature and particularly painful manner in which their death would occur, but in the failure of a new generation to be born, to enjoy the fruits of what previous generations have created, and to carry on their work.

The heart of the tragedy would be the interruption and termination of the human career and the terrible waste of potentialities that this would entail. The music of Bach would no longer be heard, the plays of Shakespeare no longer read or seen, and the knowledge mankind has laboriously acquired of the composition of the stars and the atom no longer transferred to eager and curious minds; nor would any new knowledge be acquired or new art created; no thrilling chess games would be played nor mountains admired, climbed, or skied down; no great vintages would be savored; no lovers would embrace; no children would be brought forth; no acts of kindness, justice, and mercy would occur; and no meetings for worship would be held. These are, of course, almost random examples; all the values that man has created and which give worth, above that of mere life and sentience, to human existence would cease to be experienced. And this waste, this nonfulfillment of the best that we know to exist, would be tragic.

It is simply not true that if there were no humans left to appreciate the tragedy, it would cease to be tragic. Human values have been created by generations of hard-pressed men and women, striving to hold off starvation, disease, and attacks by wild beasts and by their own kind and to create warmth, beauty, significance, truth, utility, and nobility that would endure and make life more worthwhile. The loss of all this, the disappointment of these hopes, the betrayal of all these sacrifices—if all this is not tragic, what in the world is?

This disappointment of hopes, this waste, this elimination of the possibility of valuable experience would be real, even if finally there were no people left to be aware of it.

The tree falling in the remote virgin forest creates a sound even if there is no one to hear it—the sound being the air wave that would be identified as sound by a normal eardrum in a healthy person if one were present. Similarly, the end of our race would be tragic because the loss of all these potential experiences of good would sadden most human consciences if they could know of it and could become fully aware of what was being lost.

In my observation many people consciously or unconsciously assume that we are adequately protected by supernatural powers—by Divine Providence. But orthodox religionists are more likely to find eschatological doctrines in their religions than assurances of eternal life for mankind on earth. None deny that human free will may wreak fearsome destruction, and we know that in fact some earlier civilizations have destroyed themselves—with only a fraction of the destructive capabilities that we control.

In any case many religions seem to relegate man's earthly fate to a position of secondary importance in view of the promise (or threat) of eternal life beyond the grave. And some Eastern religions may even consider conscious life, and concerns about preserving it, as itself a hindrance to the achievement of a state of transcendent bliss. Most faiths, however, address themselves to life in this world as well as in the next, and the lessons they teach about caring for others should contribute to believers' concern for social regeneration and renovation.

As I see it, the emergence of man and his culture, by means of which a part of the universe achieves self-awareness and self-expression, fulfills a basic cosmic purpose and deserves our loyalty and support. But we have no supernatural guarantees against coming to harm. Divine intervention works through human agencies. The blind faith that Providence will protect us from harm even if we fail to adapt to the changing requirements for survival is surely blind. But a belief that "God helps those who help themselves" and a sense of gratitude for our awareness, in time, of what changes are necessary can help give us the strength and determination to make the difficult changes required.

But let us suppose that mankind were in fact destroyed. Would that necessarily be the end? Could not a new (and possibly better) race of humans arise on the ashes of the old? Offhand, it seems unlikely—especially on a planet gutted of the resources required for the early stages of development. Even if it could, it very well might not reestablish contact with our own cultural tradition: Bach and Shakespeare might still be lost. Moreover, to have to go through the blood, sweat, and tears of evolution, barbarism, and development all over again, in order merely to get back in the end to where we already are now, would be tragedy enough. In any case there is no particular reason to suppose that a future sentient race would face the problems of survival any better than we are now doing. These problems, as we shall see, are not accidental or superficial but lie deep in our evolutionary history and in the limited resources of the earth. Another race that retraced our evolution would ultimately confront essentially the same problems. We are as capable of solving them as another race like ours would be, and only we can ensure the survival of *us*! It is irresponsible to beguile ourselves with the notion that somehow the human race may be given a second chance of survival—posthumously.

Some will argue, however, that human survival is a hopeless goal in any case, since sooner or later our race is doomed to expire with the cooling or overheating or explosion of the sun and the destruction of our solar system. On the basis of our present scientific information, the very long-term outlook is, admittedly, not encouraging. As presently conceived, the distances of interstellar space, the human life-span, and the speed of light impose constraints that seem to render unlikely the successful transfer of human society to new abodes in other solar systems—even though the probabilities are high that somewhere other environments congenial to human life exist and the nearest star (other than our sun) is only five light years away. But much of what we now think we know about the nature of the universe will undoubtedly turn out to be partly false: some of the fixed points and assumed certainties of contemporary science will surely crumble in time. Science after all is still in its infancy: most of the scientists who ever lived are alive today. What millions of years of additional research and development at anything like present (or possibly much higher) levels of activity could accomplish we can not as yet remotely conceive. It seems entirely possible that some day spaceships, equipped with self-sufficient human communities and permanent life-support systems and carrying records of all mankind's scientific and cultural achievements, could leave our solar system permanently in search of new worlds where human life could be transplanted and that one or more of them might achieve their goal.

But even if it turns out that in the end mankind can never really get out of the deathtrap of this solar system, or if the universe as a whole is fated to run down through entropy, disintegrate into cosmic dust, or collapse into a black hole, or if mankind and human culture must inevitably disappear in some distant future, this hardly destroys the validity of a concern for the survival of our species over the next few million years. A tragedy long deferred is, to an extent, a tragedy minimized; and a species that had fully developed and long enjoyed its highest potentialities might take its leave with less fierce regrets and sense of tragedy than one whose career had barely begun. (Certainly we feel this to be true in the case of the individual.) Moreover, there is a very great difference between unavoidable destruction from external forces and avoidable self-destruction from unimaginativeness, stupidity, and inflexibility. The most poignant tragedies are those in which a fatal flaw in the protagonist actively precipitates his own downfall—as the tragedians of ancient Greece knew full well. The self-destruction of mankind would be the most poignant tragedy of all.

I concede, of course, that no one can be forced to admit this by merely rational arguments. Some may sincerely differ. But I suspect the motives of most who profess not to care about humanity's future. Their unconcern may stem from a desire to appear profound or up-to-date or may reflect a pique that the world has given them less than they fancy they deserve or has permitted the destruction of persons or ideals they loved.

Still, it also cannot be doubted that some people are genuinely indifferent or hostile to human values and truly feel that they themselves, other people, or mankind as a whole would be better off dead, or at least no worse off. Whatever the source of such attitudes, it seems clear that they are abnormal and not truly reflective of the potential for happiness of most men and women.

It is fashionable today, no doubt, in art and social comment, to take a more or less despairing view of man's capacity for happiness, even under ideal conditions. Its extreme fashionableness does not make it true. At most it expresses the failure of our present social arrangements to make many people happy and provides an intimation of more serious and widespread miseries lying ahead if we proceed along present lines.

There are some, however, who have a strong and positive sense of values (and who value life) and who, nevertheless, still wonder whether it is really rational to worry about future generations. This doubt has been excellently formulated by Kenneth Boulding:

> It is a well-known phenomenon that individuals discount the future even in their own lives. The very existence of a positive rate of interest may be taken as at least strong supporting evidence of this hypothesis. If we discount our own future, it is certainly not unreasonable to discount posterity's future even more, even if we give posterity a vote. If we discount this at 5% per annum, posterity's vote or dollar halves every fourteen years as we look into the future, and even after a mere hundred years it is pretty small—only about 1½ cents on the dollar. If we add another 5% for uncertainty, even the vote of our grandchildren reduces almost to insignificance.[1]

To be sure, Boulding's strong moral sense will not let him accept the results of his own economist's logic. "We can argue, of course," he continues, "that the ethical thing to do is not to discount the future at all, that time discounting is mainly the result of myopia and perspective and hence is an illusion which the moral man should not tolerate."[2]

I agree with Boulding's ethical argument except that he has somewhat overstated it. I think there is nothing morally wrong with time discounting, if we use it for the sort of limited purpose for which it was originally designed. If we want to know how much extra butter on our bread next year will compensate us for eating our bread unbuttered this year, time discounting may be an appropriate procedure to use. It can help us maximize average butter consumption over a lifetime, if we are sure that that is what we really want to do. But it cannot even tell us whether we should take the risk of indigence in our old age for the sake of maximum *average* consumption over our whole life—let alone whether we should set something aside for our children. Time discounting is not capable of making moral choices between two different individuals—even between the two different individuals represented by myself today and by myself many years hence. If the rights of the second of these individuals are to be safeguarded, it must be done on the basis of a moral principle that the person I shall become is a center of value of just as much importance as the person I now am and that the welfare of that future person is not less important—just because he is not yet here, so to speak. The person I shall become may be sufficiently different from the person I am now so that I am not morally entitled to sacrifice his welfare freely and without limit in order to add to the satisfactions of the present moment, since I cannot be sure that the person I shall become would freely consent to such sacrifices at that time. It is this notion that, for example, justifies compulsory pay deductions for old-age pensions.

The principle is even clearer when it is a matter of achieving my welfare at the expense of a completely different person. Obviously, the fact that the person is a long way into the future does not make any fundamental difference, and for this reason discounting the welfare of future generations is morally wrong.

But what of discounting for uncertainty, in recognition that it is rational to make allowance for the fact that the further into the future we attempt to predict, the larger the number of the uncertainties and unforeseen contingencies and the less likely it is that our predictions will be accurate? Certainly some allowance must be made for this factor, but we must not exaggerate the degree of uncertainty in order to absolve ourselves from responsibility for acting on the basis of reasonable probabilities and existing trends. We must not confuse a lack of knowledge of the effects with a knowledge of lack of effects—as we often do. And where we know that a given trend will ultimately become harmful, even though we are not sure at exactly what level, or exactly how long it will take, we ought not to dismiss it from our minds as currently irrelevant. We must bear in mind that if the trend is maintained, the *risk* of damage will presumably increase, as will the costs of installing and operating the necessary controls to change the dangerous trend in time. In such a case, discounting for uncertainty may merely cover up a disinclination to cope with the problem in our generation and a willingness to transfer the burden to future generations.

SPATIAL VERSUS TEMPORAL EQUALITY

The present generation has developed a great passion for equality. But it is confined to spatial equality, equality of persons living at the same time in different places. It evinces, however, almost no concern for temporal equality, the equality of people living at different times, and particularly the equality of opportunity between ourselves and future generations. As we shall see, we are daily wasting for trivial purposes the nonrenewable resources that our descendants will require for their most basic needs and, simultaneously, creating problems of pollution (especially thermal pollution) that could ultimately destroy them. We do this because we happen to be here first and are willing to disregard temporal equality completely.

Let us suppose, however, that spatial and temporal equality are in conflict. Is not the first more important? I think not. If the race survives, it can steadily work toward greater spatial equality. If it does not, why bother? Even if spatial equality could be achieved for a brief instant before mankind's extinction, what lasting benefit would be derived? In fact, however, some of the measures required for temporal equality would contribute powerfully to spatial equality as well—more powerfully than most of the measures aimed directly at that objective.

If, as I have argued, our present economy sacrifices the welfare of future generations for that of the present generation, this involves a kind of exploitation. Unfortunately, our sociopolitical regulatory system has little time dimension. The protection of future generations through conservation and pollution regulation has hardly begun. (For that matter, our system does not even protect the present generation over time. It permits continuous robbing of the real value of savings and fixed incomes by means of inflation, with no legal recourse whatever.) As we shall see, a political system that depends on the intelligent use of the ballot to safeguard and balance the interests of rival groups suffers from a serious weakness in protecting the interests of those who, being still unborn, have no vote and do not even remind us of themselves by their presence as helpless children.

Sociological studies have demonstrated that we are more seriously concerned with minor tragedies next door than with major catastrophes on the other side of the world. There is a powerful weakening effect of distance on our concern for others. Our sensitivity and concern varies with physical and social distance. Clearly, the same phenomenon is true of time. As this book will show, we remain relatively indifferent to the likelihood of major tragedy for our children's children while strongly resisting the small immediate sacrifices and changes in our habits that could forestall such tragedies.

Men have always condemned a lack of elementary loyalty to one's society and descendants. Each of us is the beneficiary of the material and spiritual culture assembled over many generations by the efforts of his predecessors. To fail to conserve this and hand it on to our successors smacks of selfishness and immorality. Historically, such a policy has been openly professed only by absolute autocrats who felt that they did not require the approval of their subjects to retain power. In the modern world the same basic policies may be rationalized as we have explained—in terms of the uncertainty of the future and the urgencies of the present.

In the present day, such escapism may also be rationalized by using the current stereotypes of intergenerational conflict. The old may say: "Why should we have to worry about the young? They have it soft compared with our life when we were young. We went through the Depression [or the war, et cetera], and now inflation has robbed us of our savings. At this stage, we deserve some consideration." The young, in turn, may follow the line: "This is a world we never made. We have absolutely no responsibility for the mess things are in and will not lift a finger to save it."

There will never be a time when it will be impossible to find plausible excuses for not confronting difficult and disagreeable issues. But the longer decisions are postponed, the more agonizing the problems will look and the harder it will be to face them. The built-in hostilities between generations provide no valid excuse for either of them to sacrifice the welfare of the *next* generation. Here, if anywhere, they should find grounds for cooperation rather than conflict.

Some who concede that perhaps morally we ought to be concerned about our descendants argue that it is not realistic. We are under such awful day-to-day pressure— achieving each day's goals and averting each week's and each month's crises—that we simply have no time or energy left over to worry about the long-term future.

This is a sincere and highly plausible argument. Unfortunately, it is also culture-bound and superficial. It fails to recognize that most of the feverish day-to-day activity reflects the very policies and values that imperil human survival—the emphasizing of personal, partisan, national, and ideological rivalries and the acquisition of status and triumph symbols. If these goals could be changed, then there would be time to consider the future and to adopt policies that would make it more secure. But so long as we continue with present policies and values, we will be forever locked (through lack of time to contemplate changes) into a system that ensures our ultimate destruction. Governments in particular have been so organized and structured that, though they are nominally responsible for the long-run welfare of their citizens, they deal almost exclusively with short-range issues, attracting people who are avid for power and who, having achieved power, devote themselves to putting out already visible fires and triumphing over rivals, thereby enhancing their immediate reputations and further strengthening their political positions.

The practical political difficulty of human survival programs is that they would require the adoption of some currently unpopular measures for which there is no apparent short-term need. These measures need not, however, involve major sacrifices and would probably be consistent with rising average standards of welfare. Most men would probably accept them gladly, if persuaded that they were essential for the race's survival—considering such survival self-evidently desirable. It is practical issues of this sort (the nature and extent of the dangers to survival and the measures required to deal with them) that I shall now explore in this book.

NOTES

1. Kenneth E. Boulding, "The Economics of the Coming Spaceship Earth," in *Environmental Quality in a Growing Economy*, ed. Henry Jarrett (Baltimore: Johns Hopkins University Press, 1966), p. 12.

2. Ibid., p. 12.

2
The crisis of human survival

Man has become an endangered species. If things continue along present lines, we will probably be extinct within three centuries at the most. In any case our civilization will be destroyed, and most of us will perish miserably. Yet this need not happen. We have the will to survive and the tools of foresight and flexibility of response that have enabled us to surmount previous crises. Nor is this crisis necessarily more difficult than the others. Indeed, I think we already see the outline of a satisfactory solution. What is so difficult about this crisis is that it results from our unprecedented successes up to date, which have given us domination over all other advanced life forms (except possibly the insects). It is hard to imagine that this sort of progress, pushed even further, could create catastrophe. But it can, and it will, unless changes are made.

Nonetheless, with these changes in our institutions and governments, progress in knowledge, technology, and levels of welfare can continue, and even accelerate, without imperiling man's survival. But before we can take these measures, we must understand the dangers we face. So let us at least dare to look at what threatens us.

THE EXPONENTIAL GROWTH SYNDROME

When my great-grandparents were born, early in the nineteenth century, there were about 1 billion people in the world. It had taken about 3.5 million years* for the world's population of *Homo erectus* to grow that large—which works out to an average increase of fewer than 300 persons a year up to that time, that is to say, virtual stability.

When I became a teenager in the early 1920s, the earth's population passed the 2 billion mark. It had taken only a bit over a century to add the second billion—which works out to an average increase of nearly 9 million a year. Now, barely more than a half century later, the population has grown not merely by another 1 billion but by over 2 billion—which works out to an average increase of around 40 million a year. And our present 4.25 billion threatens to become over 5 billion in a decade, at the end of which population would be increasing by 120 million a year, an increase equal to the whole population of the United States every two years.[1]

Obviously, this exponential increase cannot continue forever. The only significant questions are How long it will continue? and What will make it stop? Actually, the second question is vastly the more important. Some expect a catastrophic rise in the death rate from famine, war, and disease. Some (especially the governments of developing countries that want to justify their neglect of population problems to concentrate entirely on industrialization) profess to believe that a demographic shift will occur whereby

---

*In 1975 Dr. Mary Leakey found the bones of 11 hominids at Laetolil near the Olduvai Gorge that were between 3.35 and 3.75 million years old. And Bryan Patterson found a hominid jaw that was 5.5 million years old.

rising living standards and lower death rates will bring about a purely spontaneous decline in birthrates, large enough to stabilize populations. My own view is that the only way to avert a catastrophic rise in death rates is for governments to reverse their existing pronatalist policies, originally formed when large populations were required for power, security, and prestige.

However, these are matters I shall discuss later. I introduce the topic of population here simply as a dramatic illustration of exponential growth. It shows very convincingly that any magnitude that keeps doubling in shorter and shorter periods of time and increasing in the absolute numbers added in a given time period must after a while collide with the limited dimensions and resources of a finite world.

Exponential growth, of course, applies not merely to population but also to the production of agricultural and industrial goods to meet the needs and wants of the enlarged population—especially in light of the revolution of rising expectations. Rising output and consumption imply, in turn, exponentially rising use of resources (e.g. energy, metals, et cetera) serving as inputs to production—this despite technological progress in recycling and more efficient use of materials and energy, which may reduce the amount of virgin raw materials and energy per unit of final output. The exponential growth of production and consumption also creates an exponential rise in pollutants from the waste products of production and consumption.

Here again, pollution controls may help retard the exponential growth of pollutants—though often at an additional cost in energy and raw materials, which, incidentally, create some additional pollution indirectly. But the initial progress through pollution control will ultimately be more than offset as the volume of waste products continues to grow exponentially, since more and more components originally recycled and purified by nature will finally be produced in such large quantities as to overwhelm the natural purifying-recycling process and will have to be artificially treated, recycled, or, at least, relocated. This takes raw materials, capital, and labor and ultimately could require a major part of economic activity. Yet if neglected, it could cause serious illness, suffering, and death.

Moreover, at least one form of pollution, waste heat, may not be controllable at all. It increases with the increased use of fossil and nuclear fuels. It could be curbed only by a massive shift over to direct and indirect forms of solar energy. We do not yet know for sure whether we could in this way obtain sufficient net energy—over the direct and indirect investment of energy inputs to get it to replace the fossil and nuclear energy we are now using and will then be using. Unless we can, or unless we curtail growth, waste heat will make the world unlivable within 200 or 300 years at the most.

To be sure, there are a number of economists, scientists, engineers, et cetera who allege that we can find substitutes for whatever is scarce and keep pollution under control for 2 to 3 percent of the GNP. I shall discuss these matters in the next chapter. Here, let me mention only one calculation I made. I found that if we increased the amounts extracted from the earth of the chief minerals by only 3 percent a year, within 1,000 years we would be extracting more than the total weight of the earth each year. Thus, obviously, there are limits. Whether we reach them a few hundred years sooner or later is not a fundamental matter of principle. If we have to adjust to limits anyhow, it may make sense to do so soon enough to give ourselves a reasonable safety margin and to leave enough for coming generations, so that they could have a reasonable chance of survival under tolerable conditions of life.

Some think that such problems can be ignored because technology will always find new ways to cope with any difficulties we encounter. This sort of blind faith in technology is an important part of the exponential growth syndrome. It provides the misplaced confidence to persevere in exponential growth, despite the obvious difficulties and risks it will create, secure in the supposed knowledge that whatever goes wrong there will always be a technological solution that will emerge in time to fix it.

In reality, however, as we shall see, such growth cannot continue indefinitely—not in a world of limited size, with a limited amount of fertile land, a limited supply of irreplaceable natural resources, and limited potential for dissipating and neutralizing the pollution engendered by human activities. At some point it simply *has* to overshoot the carrying capacity of the environment and collapse. Science and technology can help to push back these limits, but science and technology themselves can progress at only a limited speed, and they often solve certain problems only at the expense of exacerbating others (for example, lowering deaths from contagious diseases but raising the deaths from diseases based on inadequate nutrition; making it possible to utilize lower-grade materials by means that add to pollution; reducing pollution by using up more irreplaceable sources of energy; and, above all, increasing food production by means that destroy the natural fertility of the soil and the natural enemies of food predators, or that increase the vulnerability of crops by monoculture, or that expand the area of cultivation into areas of undependable climate or water supply).

The *exponential growth syndrome*, as I use the term, refers to the approach of a critical unstable phase in the three-sided relationship among uncontrolled exponential growth, the limits on growth set by the environment, and the speed with which science and technology can push back these environmental limits on growth. This critical unstable phase is reached when science and technology can make the continuation of exponential growth possible only by adopting temporary expedients that undermine the capability of the environment to support continuing growth in the next time period and that, therefore, avoid trouble now only at the expense of piling up more trouble later, by allowing growth to proceed faster than the long-term capacity of the environment to sustain growth.

This is precisely the dilemma we are now in. We are still able to continue unrestricted growth for a while, thanks to the progress of technology. But every year of such growth risks intensifying the ultimate catastrophe, when an ever-growing population with an ever-higher and more extravagant set of living standards can find no technological fix for some drastic shortage or dangerous pollutant. And, as I shall now show, when that time comes, groups of power- and prestige-seeking individuals will have instruments of fantastic destructiveness at their command, by means of which they may seek to solve their problems through coercion or threat.

THE QUANTUM JUMP IN POWER

The achievement of sophisticated nuclear weapons systems represents one of the really decisive revolutions of human history. Taking into account radiation as well as blast effects, improved speed and accuracy of delivery systems using inertially guided intercontinental missiles, and techniques for saturating or jamming potential defenses as well as hardening, hiding, or moving the launching sites, there has been achieved in a remarkably short period a multiplication of human destructive capacity by an extraordinarily high order of magnitude—possibly on the scale of hundreds of thousands or millions. This big and sudden a change completely outranks anything in previous human experience. It is something like the order of the size of change when a red giant shrinks to a neutron star or like the increase in the complexity of life forms represented by the evolution of the human brain.

The relatively trivial increase in weapon power represented by the introduction of gunpowder, muskets, and the cannon was enough to undermine European feudalism. To me, it seemed clear from the beginning that the quantum jump in destructive power represented by nuclear weapons would sooner or later make our existing nation-state system an anachronism.[2]

To be sure, just the opposite seems to have been

happening up to now. The number of sovereign nation-states has about tripled, and ethnic, linguistic, and other minorities in many countries seek to secede and form still more nations. Actually this is not surprising. With such enormous powers potentially within their grasp, ambitious groups everywhere seek to become governments, and when existing governments are beyond their reach, they seek to form new ones based on separatist sentiments and alleged grievances.

Moreover, the balance of nuclear terror has so far made it possible for minor powers to fight limited wars with considerable freedom. The mantle of sovereignty assumed by national leaders gives them moral absolution for whatever they do, since the use of weapons is automatically assumed to serve the interest of the nation—even if, in effect, it serves no more than the personal ambitions or vengefulness of leaders.

So far the system has produced no widespread conflagration. This, however, should not make us complacent. It was true also that for several years Hitler's rearmament created no particular damage. Certain processes that are apparently harmless for a time will create grave damage once they are completed. As we shall see, processes are at work that are undermining the popular balance of terror and are thereby threatening even the precarious stability we have enjoyed so far. Even this stability should not be exaggerated.

The key point about nuclear weapons is that they make it possible for a small group, aiming at world domination and daring to accept the necessary risks (which have always been high), to start a process of threat or direct menace or disruption, which if it misfires could bring about the sudden death of at least a large part of humanity and, perhaps, the lingering death of the rest. (Let there be no doubt, by the way, that such would be the results of any major nuclear exchange. While a 1975 National Academy of Sciences report, *Long-Term Worldwide Effects of Multiple Nuclear Weapon Detonations,*[3] came to relatively optimistic conclusions about the survival of at least part of the world's population, the report overlooks entirely the effects of the breakdown of economic and social institutions, the fact that the bulk of the world's grain exports come from North America, where the damage would be worst, and the fact that the thinning of the ozone layer would make it impossible to conduct farming, anywhere on earth, more than ten minutes at a time without suffering crippling sunburns and probable carcinogenic trauma.) This is the best-known and largest single threat to human survival.

Moreover, the risks that political leaders who control this capability are prepared to run may well increase over time, particularly as new people inherit or appropriate this power and as the power is diffused to more and more governments, most of them despotic and with very limited experience and judgment.

To be sure, the limited arms control achieved and the abatement of the cold war, with the beginnings of Soviet-U.S. technical and economic cooperation, are to be welcomed. But it would be serious self-deception to assume that anything accomplished so far, or prospective, provides any significant assurance against a nuclear war. (Not even 100 percent nuclear disarmament would do that, since once war started there would be a race to see who could quickest manufacture nuclear weapons again.) Even the so-called balance of terror is growing unstable. The enormous technological progress in accuracy of delivery of nuclear warheads plus the great proliferation of warheads and inexpensive low-flying delivery vehicles, which is now coming very close to us, is reviving hopes of a first-strike capability, with all the instability this brings. The other destabilizing force is the widespread distribution of nuclear materials and know-how upon which a nuclear weapons capability could be built.

This sort of danger will be enormously increased if the United States and its allies go on to what is sometimes called a plutonium economy, involving a transition from the light-water nuclear reactor to a breeder reactor, which generates large amounts of weapon-grade plutonium, and if (to earn foreign exchange) they sell plants to nonnuclear powers for processing spent nuclear fuel rods, which would also produce enough plutonium for at least a limited number of nuclear weapons (requiring, it is believed, only 20 pounds of plutonium per weapon).* While nominal safeguards exist against the diversion of such plutonium into unauthorized weapons use, they have hitherto proved quite ineffective. And as the amounts used increase, we must accept a similar growth of risk. In view of the awesome power plutonium can yield, it will undoubtedly inspire highly ingenious and forceful attempts to divert, steal, hijack, or otherwise obtain supplies. (By way of comparison, bear in mind that trading in heroin has been against the law and subject to heavy penalties in the United States for the last 20 years; yet, though motivated solely by extra-high profits, it has proved impossible to suppress or even curtail.)

Thus, even if détente can be maintained, we face a period of increasing risks, as more powers obtain nuclear arms of some sort, as the techniques of using nuclear threats are learned, and as an unfounded confidence is developed that one can reliably appraise the degree of risk invoked in various degrees and types of confrontation.

These risks are likely to mount as these powers pass into newer, less experienced, and more fanatic and unscrupulous hands and as the increasingly severe pressures of shortages of food and essential materials seem more and more to justify attempting to use these powers. Similarly, the possession of such powers may embolden a country or group of countries controlling the bulk of the world's remaining output of a high grade of a given commodity to impose a quite unconscionable price for the commodity—

---

* This whole procedure would become unnecessary if a proposal of the U.S. Arms Control and Disarmament Agency were accepted and if the spent fuel rods, instead of being reprocessed, were utilized for further power generation in the Canadian-type heavy-water reactors—after which there would be little plutonium left in the fuel rods, and they could be safely and economically treated as other nuclear wastes.

threatening nuclear countermeasures in the event of military intervention.

And, in the end such weapons could even end up in the hands of terrorist or criminal cliques. As Fred Ikle, the head of the U.S. Arms Control and Disarmament Agency, put it:

> Imagine the morning after a nuclear explosion that has destroyed half an American city. How are we going to apply our theories of mutual deterrence, of first strike, and second strike, of strategic stability conceived for a bipolar world, if we cannot tell whose nuclear explosive it was? Or even if we could tell, but it turned out to be an organization such as might exist in the future—an organization perhaps with dedicated people but no clearly defined national territory—what good then would our more than 2000 nuclear missiles and bombers do? [4]

As a postscript, it should be noted that the quantum jump in power has taken place with regard not only to weapons but also to electronic means of communication, surveillance, and recording, which can vastly increase the power of government over the individual. While democratic governments may restrain themselves in the use of these powers, tyrannies (which vastly outnumber the democracies) will not.

Radio and television make it increasingly easy, using Madison Avenue techniques for manipulating the unconscious, to control people's ideas and their behavior. Electronic technology also makes it easy to intercept messages and to identify individuals the government distrusts or wants to harrass in some way. (And Watergate was a case in point. Watergate did not show that you could not get away with it, only that you could not get away with it if you made and retained damning evidence of your own lawbreaking. This is hardly likely to happen a second time.)

What is more, that apotheosis of electronics, the computer, can easily serve as an omniscient instrument of social control by storing and instantly retrieving the dossiers of all persons who might be suspected of being in opposition to the government. In an emergency this greatly facilitates rounding them up and putting them either in preventive detention, concentration camps, or cemeteries, so that they are unable to organize any substantial resistance to any decisions the government has made.

Such social control, the essentials of which were foreseen in *1984*,[5] adds a sinister dimension to the vastly enhanced power of weaponry. In effect it is now possible for those persons planning to use force (directly or indirectly, openly or in a concealed fashion) to concentrate the decision-making process in an extremely small number of people (possibly only one) and to keep one's own people (that is, those who are still alive and in communication with others) ignorant of, or approving of, whatever decision has been, or will be, made.

THE DISINTEGRATION-ALIENATION PROCESS

In the bicentennial year of the United States, there was a natural desire to see things in as favorable a light as possible. Nevertheless, there was a notable lack of ebullience; a feeling of "decline and fall" pervaded the air. One eminent historian even explicitly drew the analogies between our situation and that of postrepublican Rome.

The average person is at least aware of growing economic insecurity, with high unemployment and a high inflation rate threatening us at the same time. He is also more or less conscious of the weakening of our community, of religion as an important influence, and even of the family. He is well aware of the rapid growth of drug addiction and crime. Moreover, in the wake of the various illegal acts of the government in Vietnam, Watergate, and the day-to-day functioning of Congress, much of the electorate is disgusted with the whole political process.

This is especially the case with those who have viewed

the quick establishment of spatial equality, in the sense set forth earlier, as the overwhelming social priority and who feel betrayed by the limited and token successes so far achieved.

Whether or not independently, there has been a vast expansion in individual alienation. It takes a variety of forms, from the simple misery of what sociologist Philip Slator calls the pursuit of loneliness[6] to the phenomenal dropout rate and the incidences of alcoholism, drug addiction, crime, nihilism, and revolutionary terrorism. Except for the purely economic aspects (of unemployment, inflation, and equality), no clear-cut cures are visible. At best one can hope that basic economic improvements, plus a few general suggestions, may be able to turn the situation around.

Most of these evils have long existed. Why at this stage should they be viewed as threatening human survival? To be sure, the direct threat seems small. There is always the possibility—but it is a faint one—that if things continue to get worse along these lines, our whole society might fall apart, like Rome in its decadence, and in its internal squabbles and wars in some way destroy itself—and at the least be taken over by some analogue of Rome's barbarians. By far the greater danger is that our internal unhappiness and dissidence would attract so much of our attention that it would leave far too little to concentrate on the long-run problems discussed in the first part of this chapter, upon the solution of which our survival *does* depend. To survive a million years, one must first survive 50. The process described here, if not arrested, could be our dominant preoccupation in the coming years. If so, we might not get around to a serious consideration of our basic long-term problems until we had passed the point of no return. Thus, indirectly, it becomes a part of the survival crisis.

NOTES

1. See *World Population Estimates, 1975* (Washington, D.C.: Environmental Fund, 1975), prepared under the direction of

Robert C. Cook, former president of the Population Reference Bureau. The estimates suggest that the rate of increase may still be increasing: it was 2.2 percent in 1975 compared with 2 percent from 1958 to 1963. However, there are also some signs that the growth rate may be leveling off. Notwithstanding popular impressions, there are no signs that the growth rate is yet declining, let alone that zero growth is remotely in sight. Even in the United States, the growth rate is still 1 percent, and there are strong indications that the recent sharp decline in fertility rates will soon be partially reversed.

2. Emile Benoit, "An American Foreign Policy for Survival," *Ethics* 56 (July 1946): 280; idem, "Control of Atomic Energy by the United Nations," *Antioch Review* 6 (Fall 1946): 488. Writing of the former article, Edward S. Corwin of Princeton said that from this article the world federalists "seem to me to have taken the main features of their program"; see Edwin S. Corwin, *A Constitution of Powers in a Secular State* (Charlottesville, Va.: Michie, 1951).

3. National Research Council. Committee to Study the Long-Term Worldwide Effects of Multiple Nuclear Weapons Detonations, *Long-Term Worldwide Effects of Multiple Nuclear-Weapons Detonations* (Washington, D.C.: National Academy of the Sciences, 1975).

4. Fred C. Ikle, "The Worldwide Spread of Nuclear Technology," Speech to the National Security Industrial Association, Jan. 15, 1975 (City: U.S. Arms Control and Disarmament Agency, Doc. 75-1), p. 8.

5. Eric Blair [George Orwell], *1984* (London: Secker & Warburg, 1949).

6. Philip Slator, *The Pursuit of Loneliness: The American Culture at the Breaking Point* (Boston: Beacon Press, 1970).

3
The coming age of shortages

Our bicentennial celebrations are now finished. I suspect that future historians will regard the past two centuries as notable not so much for the emergence of the United States as a military power, or even for its industrial predominance, but for the pervasive influence of its extravagant way of life, based on the illusion that we live in a world of plenty, with no significant limits on available resources. It looks as if the *next* two centuries will be enormously different.

The illusion of plenty as the normal state of mankind appears to be a result of two unique events of modern history, which have been misunderstood as being typical and repeatable. The first was the throwing open of the vast fertile lands of North and South America and Oceania, which quite suddenly increased our food supplies in a way not paralleled since the transition from a hunting to an agricultural economy. The second was the large-scale tapping of fossil fuels, which gave us a far more concentrated and essentially inexpensive form of energy than was ever previously available. This was especially true of oil and gas—much of which, incidentally, happened to lie in colonial or neocolonial areas where political pressures or bribery could be used to obtain them at very little above their bare costs of extraction.

This remarkably cheap energy made it economical to mine deeper and extract and refine lower-grade ores, thereby keeping down the relative cost of a wide range of raw materials. It also led to the widespread substitution of mechanical for human energy in industry and to a rapid increase in the use of physical energy and artificial chemical inputs in agriculture—to power agricultural machinery and transport agricultural products and for chemical fertilizers and insecticides.

We have now reached the point in U.S. agriculture where we use 80 gallons of gasoline or its equivalent to raise an acre of corn but only nine hours of human labor per crop acre for the average of all types of produce.[1] U.S. farm productivity looks extremely high in terms of output per man hour but not in relation to energy inputs. If, as I shall argue, energy inputs have been priced artificially and unsustainably low, it may be that we have an entirely exaggerated idea of the ease with which food can be produced in the long run and of our ability to sustain increases in population.

For the time being, however, these developments raised millions of people well above the subsistence level for the first time in history, and even made a few people affluent. The illusion that all men could be affluent—no matter how many of them—grew so that it finally became accepted as reality. Poverty was interpreted as the result of personal incompetence, misfortune, or exploitation—or as a transitional condition that the poorer countries or areas would soon overcome by the further process of "development."

Actually, while average incomes improved and a small minority became affluent, the rapid growth of population produced more and more half-starving, illiterate and ill people in the world. According to a World Bank study there were, a few years ago, some 800 million people in the world barely subsisting on the equivalent of 30 cents a day, in what it called "absolute poverty." This is about as many people as there were in the whole world 200 years ago, before the so-called Age of Plenty began.

Now it seems that even the affluence of the few is threatened, as the first indications have appeared of world-wide shortages of food and energy. Government spokesmen have tried to explain these disturbing phenomena away as accidental and temporary. To be sure, accidents were partly responsible for their appearing when and where they did. And, with luck, we may expect short-term improvements in one respect or another from time to time. But the long-term trend is unquestionably toward more widespread and acute shortages, making life more and more difficult for more and more people and more dangerous for everyone. This does not mean that a doomsday debacle is inevitable. Here, however, we are concerned not with solutions but with the nature and dimensions of the problem.

Economists sometimes minimize the dangers of shortages by the esoteric way they define them. For example, Edward Mitchell in a recent study called *U.S. Energy Policy: A Primer* suggested:

> In fact if we never found another barrel of oil, or cubic foot of natural gas, or never mined another ton of coal, there would be no necessity for shortages. This observation follows from the fact that at some price the market will clear. As long as either less is demanded or more is supplied as price increases, there is some price at which supply equals demand.[2]

Thus, according to Mitchell, so long as prices are free to rise to the level that clears the market, there can be no shortages, by definition. On this basis, a famine that kills half the population would not be regarded as a food shortage, provided there were no rationing nor price controls and that those who could afford it paid a free market price for food. I need not underline the peculiarity of this usage.

For my part, I intend to use the term *shortage* in the more normal sense of a shortfall in supply below previous, or projected, or required levels, causing inconvenience or hardship. Shortages in this sense, I shall argue, do exist and threaten to become worse—whether or not markets are free.

FOOD SHORTAGES

During the 1950s and 1960s, world food production increased by one-half. This sounds pretty good. But population increased by 46 percent. So we were barely keeping ahead of the wolf. In fact we were not even doing that, since a large part of the increase in available grain was being fed to animals for meat—and it takes several pounds of grain to make one pound of meat. Since 1960 per capita meat consumption rose a fifth in the United States, a third in West Germany, nearly doubled in Italy, and more than tripled in Japan. In 34 developing countries there was an actual decline in food production per capita. The only thing that held starvation in check was $14 billion of U.S. food aid, plus small contributions from other rich countries.

In 1972 there was an absolute decline in total world food production. This led to the rapid run down of food stocks and a rapid run up of prices. Despite more or less normal harvests thereafter, the reserve stocks remain at perilously low levels, and for a variety of reasons the outlook for the next few years is somber.

The Food and Agriculture Organization of the United Nations estimates that 450 million people are now getting too few calories to keep them alive and well: in other words they are perpetually hungry or in a state of semistarvation. This figure represents more than one person out of every ten in the world.

Will continued food aid help those now hungry to cover more of their own food requirements themselves in the future? Here the outlook is discouraging. The U.S. State Department predicts for the developing countries a more than tripling of the gap between grain production and requirements in the next ten years, even if food aid continues. Most governments of developing countries (and most of their technical advisers from developed countries as well) have thought of economic development primarily in terms of industrial development. It is only relatively recently that agricultural development is being taken more seriously. But the obstacles to a rapid expansion of food production are formidable.

Good agricultural land is continually being lost through road building, the expansion of cities, soil erosion, and the spread of desert areas. Putting new land into cultivation involves heavy investment: $800 per acre (expressed in recent prices); and most of this land is less fertile or less accessible or in areas where temperature or water supply is less dependable. It even takes a lot of investment to improve the productivity of existing cultivated farmland. It is not just a matter of introducing the "miracle" seeds of the Green Revolution. It also requires improved irrigation and more fertilizers, insecticides, farm machinery (plus the gasoline to operate it), and storage and transportation equipment. Most of these are now vastly more expensive than they were even a few years ago.

One one legitimately expect, from time to time, important agricultural breakthroughs: cereal plants with a higher protein content, with higher yields, or with greater resistance to variations in temperature or moisture or to various diseases and predators, et cetera. Such miracles will in fact be needed to keep raising average agricultural productivity anywhere near as fast as population—given erosion, climatic adversities, and the rising costs of various inputs. However, the Green Revolution experience has warned us not to expect too much of such miracles. They usually involve added costs and difficulties and are most readily adopted by the more prosperous farms, which already have a relatively high productivity.

What of the much advertised possibility of supplementing food production by utilizing synthetic production under controlled conditions: of producing a large part of the world's food in food factories? Undoubtedly, there are significant possibilities here for production of proteins. But when it comes to the production of sugars, starches, and fats, it is difficult to imagine a more economical mode of production than the use of sunlight and the automatic drawing of nutrients from the soil by plants selected by mankind over thousands of years for their efficiency in this regard. While industrial techniques can certainly increase the output of food per acre of space utilized for food production, the real question is whether industrial techniques can increase the output of food per unit of all scarce inputs (energy, raw materials, capital, et cetera) utilized. The rapidly rising costs of these inputs keep reducing the practicability of this approach except for very high-priced specialty items.

As for fish, which supplies the bulk of the animal protein for many poor countries, we seem to have come close to the maximum sustainable catch (at least by present hunting, rather than farming, techniques), and even that catch is threatened by pollution and overfishing.

Moreover, a number of experts on climate believe that climatic conditions for farming are deteriorating. In recent decades the growing season in the United Kingdom has been shortened by two weeks, and other countries in the Northern Hemisphere have increasingly experienced untimely rains and premature freezes. Meanwhile, the monsoon rains upon which 300 to 400 million Africans and Asians heavily rely have become increasingly undependable. An alarming fact is that the permanent ice cover of the globe suddenly expanded by one-eighth in 1971-72 and has not yet receded.

Putting all these factors together, it looks as though continuing to increase food production may become extremely difficult and expensive. But the number of people that have to be fed increases every year—by 80 million a year (more in three years than the whole population of the United States). Obviously, there is no way of adding, correspondingly, to the land area of the globe—or of even putting that much additional land into cultivation. And it is now becoming far more difficult and expensive to find the investment and the additional inputs to raise the productivity of land already in cultivation.

ENERGY SHORTAGE

There is no question that the Arab-Israeli conflict precipitated the energy crisis sooner than it might otherwise have occurred. But it is a mistake to overlook the underlying economics of the energy situation, which in a fundamental sense justified the quadrupling of oil prices and made the Organization of Petroleum Exporting Countries (OPEC) realize they could sustain it.

The underlying factor here was the rapid depletion of the world's oil reserves. If consumption had continued to grow at the old rate, existing reserves would have been exhausted in around 25 years. If new finds equal to four times the present reserves could have been discovered and exploited (and recent finds in Alaska, the North Sea, Mexico, China, et cetera are not on a scale that suggests that this could be easily accomplished), this would have extended the life of the reserves only for another 25 years, approximately—assuming continuing growth in consumption at the old rate.

It was the recognition of the limited reserves available, in relation to the rapidly growing demand, that undoubtedly encouraged the producer countries to band together to collect more of the real benefits from the long-term scarcity value of the oil, while stretching out the period over which the returns could be collected. They finally realized that it was not in their interest to sell at a price that would maximize current sales and that their aim should rather be to restrict sales and maximize revenues over the whole life of their reserves.

The governments of the oil-importing countries showed no comprehension of the fact that they were facing the beginning of a long-term energy shortage and busied themselves with elaborate schemes for financing a continuing increase of imports. The name of this game was petrodollar recycling, and the essential ingredient was the development of techniques for ensuring that the oil-importing countries could borrow enough (or sell off enough of their capital assets) to continue importing the oil.

At best this provided only a temporary solution. In 1974 the OPEC countries exported $110 billion of oil. They were able to spend only $49 billion of the proceeds on their own imports and ended up with a petrodollar overhang of $61 billion in financial assets. Of this $61 billion, $38 billion belonged to six countries—Kuwait, Abu Dhabi, Qatar, Dubai, Libya, and Saudi Arabia—with a combined population of only 12 million, mostly very poor desert dwellers. They spent only $14 billion on imports.[3] They could not have spent another $38 billion without completely disrupting their normal lives.

When one thinks of the amounts likely to be involved in the years ahead—taking into consideration further price increases imposed to offset the inflationary rise in their import prices and the earnings of the reinvested earnings—the totals become positively awesome. And it is difficult to imagine that financial transfers of such magnitude can long continue without comparable international transfers of real wealth, involving the real impoverishment of some countries for the benefit of others.

Former Secretary of State Henry Kissinger said some time back that "without a new international structure, Western Civilization is almost certain to disintegrate." He has argued for a defensive cartel of oil-consuming nations to force OPEC to reduce oil prices. More recently, he has indicated an awareness that such a group would have little bargaining power unless they sharply cut back their oil consumption.

This is good advice, though it comes a bit late in the day and with no indication as to how it could be done. Moreover, the context in which it is offered makes it appear unrealistic. Essentially, it is viewed as a strategem by means of which the oil cartel may be sufficiently weakened so that prices will sharply decline—at which point the historic uptrend in oil consumption can recommence.

This seems to me wishful thinking of the most obvious sort. It vastly underrates the strength of the OPEC position and overrates the strength of our own. Even if some members of OPEC do cheat a bit by secretly cutting prices, they are likely to be the relatively smaller producers with limited capacity to expand their output. This can easily be offset by further production cuts by the biggest producers, which are least likely to have urgent uses for their petrodollar hoard. Moreover, it is only a matter of time until they come to realize that in an inflationary age their own oil in the ground is a better investment than any they can buy with the proceeds of selling it. So far, at least, the decline in consumption resulting from the world recession has not seriously corroded OPEC unity.

The point is that in 1974 OPEC countries used only 45 percent of their petrodollar earnings to finance their imports. Thus, they could have exported 55 percent less oil and still had enough to pay for all their imports. (Actually, if they had exported less, the prices would have been even higher. So they would still have earned a good deal more than they needed for their imports.)

But Japan, Europe, and the United States could *not* get along comfortably on 55 percent less oil imports. The only realistic chance they would have to cut oil imports significantly (unless faced with another embargo) is to regard the cut not as a temporary expedient, to force down oil prices, but as a part of a long-term change in their whole life-style in which they would use less energy and derive much more of it from sources other than oil. No one is going to make the major sacrifices involved in drastically cutting back energy uses temporarily to win what in the end would prove to be a temporary cut in oil prices.

For make no mistake about it, oil prices are still far too low to encourage proper conservation of this immensely precious resource or to express its true long-term value to future generations of users. Actually, petroleum is such a treasure house of organic chemicals in readily extractable form that it should probably be regarded as essentially a chemical feedstock, only the less utilizable parts of which should be used as fuel. I fear that future generations will not easily forgive us for having burned it up in so prodigal a fashion and for such trivial purposes. As these long-term considerations become more apparent, and as we come closer to the end of our reserves, petroleum prices will inevitably move higher—whatever temporary price concessions the oil-consuming countries might be able to wring out of OPEC. Thus, we shall be forced willy-nilly to admit the reality of the long-term energy shortage and to begin to make our adjustment to it. The sooner we face up to the situation and begin to work out satisfactory long-term solutions, the more likely it will be that we can avoid desperate crises and the risks of major breakdown, or even more horrible solutions.

Thus, Secretary Kissinger publicly stated that an interruption in the oil flow that led to economic strangulation could result in war. This is something that was generally realized, but the fact that Kissinger publicly acknowledged the reality was in itself significant. Indeed, this is one way that the emerging long-term energy shortage could bring about the destruction of our civilization in very short order indeed. But oil, of course, is not the only source of energy. We must now consider some of the obstacles to, and limitations of, alternative energy sources.

There are two fundamental obstacles in even getting started on the development of alternative energy sources to replace oil to any substantial extent. The first is the fantastic size of the operation and the prodigious capital investment required. This is not a purely financial matter. What is fundamentally involved in such investment is the diversion of millions of tons of steel, copper, petroleum, et cetera for the creation and operation of enormous facilities that will, in some respect, parallel the already existing oil facilities. It is extremely difficult to mobilize people to make the enormous, immediate sacrifices involved in diverting resources from other badly needed uses.

The second major obstacle is that no potential substitute promises to be anywhere near as low in cost as oil, especially Mideastern oil, which costs next to nothing to extract. So long as men remain hypnotized by the myth of cheap energy, which is so fundamental a part of the imaginary age of plenty, they cannot reconcile themselves to making enormous sacrifices to create substitute energy systems, which are bound to deliver energy at far higher costs. Unless governments can guarantee a continuing long-term market for this higher-priced substitute energy, private enterprise cannot afford to take the risks of producing it. It would be utterly vulnerable to a temporary decline in oil prices, which would destroy its markets, while still giving the low-cost oil producers a quite adequate return. Thus, only long-term purchase guarantees by governments could help. But governments, still living in the imaginary age of plenty, cannot reconcile themselves to saddling themselves with permanently high energy costs, even for a part of their energy requirements.

There are other difficulties of a technological nature. Even when a suitable technology is available, the enormous size of the operation means that at the least it would take a long time to phase it in. Moreover, none of the energy alternatives offer the prospect of a *permanent* solution to the energy problem: in the sense of satisfying all our energy needs into the distant future. An examination of some of the specific energy programs may illustrate these various difficulties and limitations.

FOSSIL FUELS

Consider first shale oil. In Colorado, Wyoming, and Utah, there are shale deposits containing an estimated 1.8 trillion barrels of oil, the best of which (in Colorado) could provide 117 billion barrels. This compares with 52 billion barrels of proved U.S. reserves of regular liquid petroleum. Why then do we have an oil shortage? Shale oil can be extracted. It has been extracted in Scotland and Estonia, and the Union Oil Company of California ran a test project successfully in the United States in 1957.

The difficulty has been in the costs. The shale was first mined, mostly deep-mined, and then heated to extract the oil. The mining and heating required much equipment and energy inputs. This reduces the net energy and net profitability of the whole process. The most serious current limitation is the water requirements—about three barrels of water for each barrel of oil produced. The water is not locally available for the production of more than 1 million barrels of oil a day (current U.S. consumption is 18 million barrels).

On-site technologies, in which the shale is burned inside the mountain and the melted oil runoff collected, offer a more promising prospect. But so far it has not proved technologically feasible to put the process on a continuously self-sustaining basis in completely on-site situations. Partial on-site techniques offer more immediate hope. The method developed by Occidental Petroleum mines a fifth to a third of the shale in the regular way, then seals off and burns the underground cavity, draining off the released oil through a previously channeled trough. However, even this technique if fully successful would take several years to put into large-scale commercial operation and might require one such excavation a week to produce 30,000 barrels of oil a day. This would be less than 2 percent of U.S. current consumption. It is quite impossible to tell what the ultimate costs would be. Thus, even at best, shale oil could be provided only at a fairly high cost and only for the medium term, not immediately. Even this will not occur unless we decide promptly to accept permanently high costs for at least part of our energy supply and to divert large amounts of capital away from other uses to obtain it.

Coal, on the other hand, is both in abundant worldwide supply and has a well-established technology for extraction and use. World reserves are estimated at an amount sufficient to supply the current rate of use for 2,700 years, and it is supposed that at least this much again may be ultimately recoverable in the top kilometer of the earth's surface. If all this coal could be extracted, it would last for over 5,000 years at the present rate of use. But if coal consumption keeps growing as in the past (at say 4.1 percent a year), it would last not 5,000 years but only 135 years! As other fossil fuels are exhausted, one might expect the rate of coal utilization to speed up rather than slow down.

Coal, of course, has well-known physical and technical limitations, which is why it has been largely displaced by oil for so many uses. It is expensive and dangerous to mine underground. And strip mining is also not inexpensive if one undertakes to restore the strip-mined land to its preexisting state. (If one does not, then one permanently loses the usefulness of the land, besides destroying its aesthetic values.) Here again, the availability of water may be the limiting factor. Moreover, combustion of coal in large quantities creates severe pollution problems, the control of which requires heavy investment in anti-pollution equipment to remove the pollutants before or after combustion. Even if the smoke is well dissipated by high chimneys, it may be carried long distances by the winds and still ultimately acidify the rain and cause major destruction of forests far from the area of emission. In addition, coal is expensive stuff to transport per British thermal unit. If turned into electricity at the mine, this involves a major loss of electricity if transmitted for long distances.

For a variety of reasons, therefore, processes for liquefying and gasifying coal are bound to attract increasing interest—even though the cost of the end product is bound to be much higher than that of natural oil and gas and though a significant fraction of the energy in the coal would have to be used up in the conversion process.

Putting all the fossil fuels together, the general conclusion seems to be as follows. Whatever we do, costs are bound to be far higher than they used to be and, despite some variations, are likely to be on an upward trend. Our pattern of life has depended on unrealistically low energy costs—to an extent we never fully realized—and it will have to be drastically changed, even in the medium term.

Moreover, if demand keeps growing as in the past, it appears that usable fossil fuel supplies will be exhausted in 150 to 200 years. More fossil fuels will probably still be buried within the earth; but it would take more energy to extract, refine, and transport them (and nullify their dangerous pollution effects) than the amount of usable energy finally delivered.

NUCLEAR POWER

For the last quarter of a century, mankind has assumed that whatever else happened on the energy front, it always had an ace in the hole, namely, nuclear energy. But today, after two decades and billions of dollars of expenditure on research and development (R&D), nuclear power plants account for only a tiny fraction even of electricity production. Moreover, many applications for the construction of additional plants have recently been withdrawn. Construction costs have risen astronomically, and while an elaborate and impressive-looking four-volume study directed by Norman Rasmussen of Massachusetts Institute of Technology (MIT) was carried out to demonstrate that the risks of dangerous accidents are statistically negligible,[4] many experts remain unpersuaded. Their reservations and doubts are lucidly summarized in two articles by John T. Edsall of Harvard in *Environmental Conservation*.[5]

Consequently, adequate insurance against the potential

liabilities, if available at all, would be prohibitively expensive, unless the plants were located in distant and inaccessible areas. If this were the case, their operating costs, including the costs of transporting the electric energy they produced to distant markets, could become quite high.

One of the more constructive suggestions I have seen to deal with this problem was in a very thoughtful article by Carroll Wilson of MIT.[6] He proposed that in order to allay some of these anxieties—whether or not well founded— future nuclear plants should be built underground. This would add somewhat to the capital costs (but not inordinately). While it would not ensure in the event of a major accident and meltdown that some of the radioactive products might not ultimately contaminate water supplies or soil within a limited area, it would greatly reduce the risk of a major uncontrollable catastrophe. The fact that so little attention has been paid to this proposal shows how completely unprepared we are psychologically to accept the inevitability of higher energy costs in the future and how fiercely we resist acknowledging that the age of scarcity has begun.

Another factor recently retarding the building of conventional nuclear reactors is the fear that they might become uncompetitive, if a new variety—the breeder reactor— might soon become available. This variety would have much lower fuel costs, since in the course of consuming fissionable uranium (which is in limited supply) it would enrich other more plentiful isotopes of uranium and thorium, transforming them into fissionable fuels.

To a layman like myself, the breeder reactor seems like the most appallingly dangerous industrial contraption ever conceived. Its main by-product, plutonium, is the most dangerous of all elements, being highly poisonous, highly corrosive, highly radioactive, and (at critical mass) highly explosive. Moreover, at least the main variety of the breeder reactor would use liquid sodium in its heat exchanger, a substance that reacts violently with any trace of moisture. Although the federal government is spending most of its nonmilitary R&D funds on the solution of these problems, it has so far failed to solve them satisfactorily—even to the point where the risk factor would be of the same order as in conventional nuclear plants.

Even if these technical difficulties could be overcome, nuclear power would not necessarily be cheap. All that breeder reactors would do is to reduce the cost of fuel. But fuel costs are only a relatively small part of the total cost of delivered, usable energy for the consumer. Because of the complexity of the process and the elaborate safety precautions required, nuclear energy can never hope to be cheap. Present costs have been artificially reduced by the implicit subsidy built into the costs of the fuel and even the reactors, since the R&D costs, the isotope separation costs, and the basic design cost of nuclear power reactors were primarily charged off to various parts of the nuclear weapons program, including nuclear submarine power plants.

Moreover, there is one built-in hazard in the development of industrial nuclear power that is hard to translate into economic terms but is very real nevertheless. It is now projected that in 20 years with the continued development of the world's nuclear energy programs, there will be enough fissionable material in international transit to make 20,000 atomic bombs. With the wide gaps that exist in the network of international controls, and the rapid diffusion of nuclear know-how, it is becoming increasingly easy to divert fissionable materials from authorized channels and to fashion them into nuclear explosives—as has been recently demonstrated by India.

As this process continues, and nuclear weapons become more and more widely diffused, the bipolar balance of terror that has so far prevented nuclear war will be undermined.

The mirage that lures us further and further along the path of nuclear power is the Faustian hope for unlimited energy from new nuclear processes. William Nordhaus of Yale has calculated on the basis of estimates of W. K. Hubbert that the breeder technology would provide mankind with energy enough for a million years and that nuclear fusion, if achieved, could provide energy for 53 billion years.[7]

The imagination of the scientific and technical community has been particularly stimulated by nuclear fusion. It seems likely that it would run minimal dangers of serious accident, would produce minimal radiation leakage, and would not require the transport and storage of dangerous large quantities of radioactive waste products with long half-lives. But will it work? Recently, the addition of laser technology to the extended prior work on plasma technology has encouraged hopes of an early breakthrough— possibly providing a demonstration of technical feasibility by the 1980s. Of course, in such matters one can never be sure until one has actually done it.

Moreover, technical feasibility would mean only that the usable energy derived would exceed the total energy inputs required to collect and purify the nuclear materials, bring about their fusion, and safely lead off the resulting energy. Economic feasibility is quite another matter: it would require that the energy created have a value well in excess of the total value of all the costs required to produce it, including not only the energy inputs but interest and depreciation on the capital invested, insurance, wages, distribution costs, et cetera.

Even if fusion energy turns out to be economically feasible, it will not necessarily be cheap. Any process utilizing temperatures (albeit intermittently) comparable with those inside the sun will inevitably be highly capital intensive. As we have previously noted, it is not the cost of the fuel that chiefly determines the cost of most forms of power but the cost of the capital required to transform the energy into usable form and deliver it to the user. While we cannot know for sure, until we find out exactly how to obtain controlled nuclear fusion, it does look as though it will be a relatively high-cost way of obtaining usable power.

But the basic long-term limitation of fusion power— as with all other forms of power based on nuclear or fossil fuels—is that it generates waste heat and tends to raise the temperature of the atmosphere. Thus, if the world continues the past rate of growth in energy utilization of around 4 percent, all talk of using the breeder reactor for a million years, or using the fusion reactor for 53 billion years, must be dismissed as completely misleading. Instead, within only 150 to 250 years—if not sooner—we would run smack into the thermal barrier: waste heat from fossil and nuclear fuels would melt the world's ice cover, resulting in the great port cities of the world being submerged; by the end of this period, the waste heat would add at least 50 degrees centigrade to the average temperature of the earth—a situation to which the human race could obviously not adapt.[8]

There is a considerable margin of error in these preliminary estimates, but the margin of error looks wide only in relation to the way we ordinarily discount the future. We are talking of what will probably happen if we pursue our present way of life for only five or ten or more generations. Now, five or ten generations is a mere moment in the whole career of mankind—and this would still be so even if it turned out to be 10 to 20 generations instead.

Nor should we forget that the large margin for error in these calculations works in both directions: conditions could easily deteriorate even faster than here estimated if, for example, the massive attempts of the developing countries to industrialize, or unexpectedly rapid progress on nuclear fusion processes, led to a speedup in the growth of fossil and nuclear energy use from 4 to 5 per cent per annum, or possibly even higher.

SOLAR ENERGY

There is only one possible exception to all this, and at this stage it isn't clear how wide an exception it might become. This is solar energy, both direct, in the form of sunlight, and indirect, in the energy stored in winds, moving water, thermal gradients in the oceans, and in organic life through photosynthesis. The use of these forms of energy does not add to the amount of waste heat in the atmosphere (though one proposed method of harnessing solar heat would be an exception to this rule: a space satellite with an array of photoelectric cells, capable of transmitting the solar energy via short waves to earth; such a satellite might capture some solar energy that would not otherwise have reached the surface of the earth, and thus might generate additional waste heat).

A considerable part of the world's potential hydroelectric energy has already been tapped, at least in the industrial areas. For other forms of solar energy, the outlook is technically or economically uncertain. The use of direct sunlight for space heating and cooling is on the verge of being economically competitive, at least in sunny climates. The production of methanol as a motor-fuel supplement and general fuel appears highly competitive, especially if it can be produced from garbage and other organic wastes. Prospects also seem favorable for greatly improved wind-powered generators that would be far more efficient than old-fashioned windmills, especially if linked up to flywheels to store the energy.

However, any large-scale substitution of solar for fossil or nuclear energy would involve enormous capital outlays. Since most forms of solar energy are relatively diffuse, elaborate equipment is required to concentrate and store it and to transform it into a usable form. This means that it is necessary to use large amounts of already existing energy to mine and refine the ores out of which the solar utilization equipment will be made, to run this equipment, and to transmit the energy to the user. Thus, the net amount of useful energy delivered by the process may be slight, probably less than that achieved by continuing to pump oil out of already drilled oil fields.

This is why, up to now, most forms of solar energy have been little developed and why some that were used in the past (like windmills) have been largely abandoned. With a major R&D effort, solar energy in various forms could certainly be much more extensively developed; but it is far from obvious that enough net energy could thereby be generated out of the current inflow of solar energy to replace the vast amounts of energy now being extracted from the already highly concentrated stored energy from the past. The trouble is that our present "energy standard of living" is based upon the using up of this accumulated store of energy inherited from the past. Up to now, it would appear to be difficult to maintain (let alone improve) that standard, if we had to rely solely on the current solar energy inflow in the diffuse form in which it arrives.

Our only chance of a truly long-range future with relatively high energy consumption is to learn to use fossil and nuclear fuels to buy us time: the time needed to learn how to use the various forms of solar energy most effectively and, thereafter, the time to construct and operate the technology for the use of solar power. The aim should be to generate enough net energy from solar processes so that it could not only cover most of our current energy requirements but also supply the additional energy needed to renew and expand the solar energy utilization equipment itself.

At this stage we cannot know whether this could ever be achieved. The only prudent course is to cut back drastically current consumption and to conserve our inherited energy stocks, so that if the net energy contribution from current solar energy inflow remains small—despite all the solar energy research we can do—we will still be able to supplement it by gradually using up our inherited energy stocks. This would enable a high level of civilization to persist for the longest attainable period.

RAW MATERIALS SHORTAGES

In addition to the shortages of food and energy that have been discussed, there are prospective shortages ahead for a variety of nonrenewable raw materials other than energy producers, such as metals, sulfur, and phosphates.

If one takes the official estimates by the U.S. Bureau of

Mines for the known reserves of the most important of these materials and calculates how long they would last, assuming a continued growth of demand in line with past long-term trends, then one comes to the conclusion that they will all be gone in a century or less. Even if one makes the apparently liberal assumption that new finds will bring the reserves up to five times their present size (or that new technologies will quintuple the amount of resources that are usable), the reserves would still be exhausted in less than two centuries.[9]

Critics, however, allege that known reserves constitute only a small part of "ultimately recoverable resources," which the U.S. Geological Survey estimates to exist in the top kilometer of the earth's crust—based on amounts already discovered in comparable geological formations. Calculated in this way, Nordhaus estimates that ultimately recoverable resources of aluminum would provide 68,066 years of consumption at the present rate. On the basis of this, and large estimates for other minerals, he concludes: "The clear evidence is that the future will not be limited by sheer availability of important materials; rather any drag on economic growth will arise from increases in costs."[10]

This could turn out to be one of the more celebrated non sequiturs in economic literature. Any attempt to measure the impact of future growth by means of a static reserve index—comparing the estimated stock of the material with the present rate of consumption—can be thoroughly misleading. For this purpose, only an exponential index will do: one that compares the estimated stock with a rate of consumption projected to continue growing in line with past trends. The difference in these two ways of measuring the adequacy of the stocks is enormous. Thus, if we assume a continuing growth in the consumption of aluminum in line with past trends (of 6.4 percent a year), then it turns out that ultimately recoverable resources would be exhausted not in 68,000 years but in 140 years.

Clearly, static indexes are utterly misleading in assessing the effects of growth: how long the stocks will last is much less sensitive to the size of the stocks than it is to the rate of growth in consumption. Because the long-term effects of sustained growth are intuitively so very unobvious (and, indeed are so hard at first to believe), it is dangerous to base policy in this field on general impressions—or even on estimates, if the assumptions on which they are based have not been systematically checked for appropriateness and consistency.

But is it realistic to assume a long-term continuation of recent trends? Any statistician will tell you that a long-term projection of recent trends is almost bound to be wrong. Here we must be careful not to misunderstand. To discover what would happen if growth did continue is not to predict that growth will continue. The purpose, indeed, may be to find out whether growth may not have to be slowed. It ill befits those who argue that continued growth is possible and desirable to object when the "unrealistic" multiplicative implications of continuing growth are pointed out.

Many economists have been critical of estimates of materials shortages that give no significant role to substitution between commodities and to the effect of prices in stimulating such substitutions and in encouraging conservation, recycling, or more exploration and intensive exploitation of commodities that are in short supply. However, if we are primarily concerned with the very long run, and with all nonrenewable resources taken as a group, then substitutions and price movements may have only a limited role. Many of the substitutes would themselves be running short; and rising prices would no longer serve to stimulate substituted or additional output but only to register the fact that irremediable shortages exist and to force catastrophic cuts in consumption. As for recycling, *The Limits to Growth* projects catastrophic shortages despite very extensive recycling, which could reduce the amount of virgin raw materials per unit of output by 75 percent.[11] (Not everything can be recycled; recycling is almost never total; and recycling takes energy.)

There is a widespread impression that the mining of the manganese nodules of the seabed may solve our raw materials problems, at least with respect to certain important nonferrous metals. According to some experts (although it is questioned by others), these nodules may in 10 to 20 years be providing copper equal to a fourth of current output, nickel equal to three times current output, and manganese equal to six times current output—with the potential of ultimately quadrupling these quantities.[12] This sounds impressive, until one realizes that if past growth trends continue, annual demand 100 years from now would be 90 times the present level for copper, 28 times the present level for nickel, and 17 times the present level for manganese. Thus, the additional quantities supplied by the nodules could significantly delay the appearance of shortages with respect to a few important minerals but could not change the essential character of the long-term depletion problem arising from continued growth of demand.

A number of economists have questioned the thesis of growing raw materials scarcity because of the lack of any evidence of it in the movement of relative prices. In essence, they ask: "If raw materials have been getting increasingly scarce, why is it that their price has not been rising relative to other things?"

Nordhaus, for example, points out that the relative price of most minerals relative to wages per hour in industry steadily declined between 1900 and 1970.[13] This is undoubtedly true, although the movement since 1970 has been in the opposite direction. But what does the increasing relative cheapness of raw materials from 1900 to 1970 really prove? Between 1900 and 1970 the labor costs of developing countries (the measure used here is based on the United States) were being driven up by trade union monopoly control over key areas of the labor market. On the other hand, the cost of materials was being held down by vast new finds of highly concentrated and easily exploitable minerals and energy (especially oil and gas) in developing countries under colonial or neocolonial governments, which were unable to limit the rate of exploitation to the degree necessary to obtain prices that would include appropriate depletion charges reflecting the long-term value of the materials to future generations.

The presence of absurdly cheap energy supplies made it possible to mine more deeply and smelt lower grades of ores without raising the cost of the refined metals by nearly as much as the price of labor was being raised by the trade union activity in developed countries. The world markets for energy and basic metals were far more competitive than the U.S. market for labor. Therefore, it was possible to raise the price of U.S. labor a lot faster than the world prices for energy and metals. But this does not mean that the available stocks of energy and metals were not being run down—as we are now beginning to realize.

The last line of defense for the cornucopian view is the existence of awesomely vast amounts of minerals thinly diffused in the earth's crust or in the seas. From this viewpoint, David B. Brooks and P. W. Anderson have argued:

> The literal notion of running out of mineral supplies is ridiculous. The entire planet is composed of minerals, and man can hardly mine himself out. . . . A single cubic kilometer of average crustal rock contains 2×10^8 (metric . . .) tons of copper. . . . We are not suggesting that such dilute material will ever be mined, but only indicating that exhaustion in a physical sense is meaningless.[14]

This is unfortunate hyperbole. The notions of literally "running out of mineral supplies" and "mining ourselves out" are by no means meaningless. Annual consumption of ten leading minerals is now about 2.7 billion tons. At even a 3 percent growth rate, in 1,000 years annual consumption would exceed the weight of the earth (6×10^{21} tons). Thus, even if the earth were made of 100 percent usable ores and energy sources, and even if recycling were extraordinarily advanced, we know that recent growth trends in mineral consumption would have to stop long before the year 2976. And between a 1,000-year maximum and, say, a 200-year minimum (based on estimated amounts of minerals likely to exist in usable concentrations), the 200-year figure is obviously a great deal closer to the ultimate limits of the achievable than the 1,000-year figure. Even 1,000 years is not eternity; it is only a quarter of recorded history.

The point is that *usable resources* in any realistic sense of the term cannot include enormous amounts of minerals in extremely diffuse concentrations. These minerals would never be economically usable unless the necessary industrial power for extraction and refinement (and for rectifying the ensuing environmental damages) were extremely cheap. If such cheap power is not going to be available, as I have argued, then the existence of these very low-grade minerals is largely irrelevant. Thus, we can continue to talk quite meaningfully about the possibility of "running out of mineral supplies," even in the relatively short term, in the elliptical sense of running out of those raw materials that would yield a higher value in refined and usable end products than the energy and raw material inputs required to extract and refine them.

POLLUTION

Growth is limited not only by the depletion of nonrenewable resources, which leads to critical shortages. It is also limited by the inevitable accumulation of waste products inimical to human welfare and disruptive of the chain of life on which human life ultimately depends.

Economists have generally viewed pollution as merely a "disamenity," a negative "externality," which should be reduced only to the point where its marginal disutility is equal to the marginal cost of the controls. But as the volume of pollution rises, it increasingly becomes a source of disease, disability, and death—the disutilities of which are not readily measurable in dollar terms.

When humanity and its economy were sufficiently small and scattered, the waste products were relatively easily dispersed and recycled by natural means, and pollution seemed a minor problem. With the massive growth of population, agriculture, and industry, the dispersal, neutralization, and recycling of by-products of human activity have become serious problems, which already cost a good deal of money. In Japan hundreds of thousands of persons have diseases believed to be pollution related. In New York taxi drivers or others spending much time in traffic already have a level of carbon monoxide in their blood that would make it dangerous to use their blood for blood transfusions to persons with heart ailments. Every year we discover new substances, many of them in wide circulation for many years, that offer serious dangers to health.

This raises grave doubts about what life would be like if the level of industrial activity and the resultant pollutants were enormously increased. For example, if world industrial growth should continue at only 4 percent (in recent decades it has been closer to 7 percent), then in 200 years industrial production would be 2,500 times the present level.

The horror of living in a hyperpolluted environment is difficult to imagine. (A vivid impression of what it might be like is conveyed in John Brunner's novel *The Sheep Look Up* [1973].) [15] Of course, some pollution would be checked by improved antipollution technology and additional antipollution equipment. But this equipment would curb only a part of the pollution and would itself pollute—that is, it would require additional inputs of energy and raw materials to produce and operate, which would generate pollution. The notion that 2 or 3 percent of the GNP could control pollution is based on projected U.S. growth alone, and for only a few decades. If the volume of world industry and its by-products increased by a really large factor, then we would find that hundreds or thousands of substances, now naturally recycled, would have passed certain critical levels and emerged as new pollutants—which we would have to identify, evaluate, and control. Some might even combine (like smog) and prove to be particularly dangerous. (Incidentally, in their eagerness to maximize development, some of the developing countries may well resist antipollution measures—for example, bans on DDT—and even deliberately set up pollution havens to attract more industry.)

Even the developed countries, faced with shortages of clean fuels, are beginning to weaken their antipollution programs, arguing that employment and growth are more important then environmental purity. What they do not recognize is that heavy pollution will in time also stop growth—perhaps not so soon but ultimately in a more traumatic manner.

TECHNOLOGY AN ESCAPE HATCH?

It is sometimes argued that energy and shortage concerns are exaggerated because technological progress will be able to solve most of the upcoming problems—averting famine by increasing plant yields, finding adequate substitutes for scarce energies and raw materials, and providing new and more ingenious equipment for pollution control and recycling.

Actually, these projections by no means ignore the helpful role of technology. We could not project continuing economic growth at former rates without implicitly assuming that technology continued to improve productivity, locate new deposits of energy and materials, develop new energy sources, reduce the amount of raw materials inputs and of pollution per unit of output, et cetera. However, even making fairly generous allowance for the contribution of technology in these fields, only a small part of the probable dangers of unlimited growth would be averted. In *The Limits to Growth* and successor studies, for example, it was assumed that new materials resources equal to four times existing reserves would be found and exploited and that conservation and recycling would reduce the amount of virgin raw material per unit of output by 80 percent, the amount of pollution per unit of output by 80 percent, and so on. Disaster was predicted despite these technological advances. If even more favorable assumptions of technological progress are made, we find that this merely delays the outcome by a small number of decades. It is partly to allow for such contingencies that I speak of the maximum period of unlimited growth as 200 years, instead of 125 years, as was done in *The Limits to Growth.*

Technology is sometimes viewed as a miraculous escape hatch that can be relied upon to substitute for any failing element in the system and to get us out of any and all problems that our negligence or mismanagement may create. Carl Kaysen wrote:

> Once an exponentially improving technology is admitted into the model, along with exponentially growing population and production, the nature of its outcomes changes sharply. The inevitability of crisis when a limit is reached disappears, since the "limits" themselves are no longer fixed, but grow exponentially, too.[16]

Such a view grossly misinterprets technology's role. What technology has chiefly done is to economize on human labor or time at the expense of nonrenewable natural resources or to substitute one such resource for another. It has also provided tools for better physical and mental performance, health, and mobility. But this has not removed or modified any natural built-in limits in the external world. It may be significant that there is now little further research on increasing the speed of message transmissions, in view of the fact that our communications are already close to the fixed speed of light and of electromagnetic impulses. Technology does not make these limits grow exponentially but accepts these limits as fixed barriers to further progress along these particular lines and shifts to other areas. Similarly, technology cannot modify the waste-heat effect of nonsolar energy use or prevent the thermal barrier from destroying mankind if sufficient waste heat is allowed to accumulate.

Technology is thus not an omnipotent force that can be counted upon to solve whatever problems we create. Nor would its exponential growth guarantee that it could solve the problems created by the exponential growth of everything else. In the first place, we must remember that most R&D is dedicated to improving our ability to kill each other and to various other matters that contribute little to our long-term survival capability. Technological progress generally creates more problems than it solves.

Thus, part of technology's growth is devoted to dealing with problems created by the growth of technology itself. By no means is all of it available to deal with the problems created by growth of the economy. A speedup in technological progress will not ensure that more technology will automatically be available for protecting the environment.

Furthermore, the exponential growth of R&D may not, in fact, continue. The R&D expenditure of the United States declined from 3.0 percent of the GNP in 1967 to 2.6 percent in 1971, and there were also declines in France and the United Kingdom. During the present recession, there have been major cutbacks not only in R&D but also in financial support for the training of scientific and technical personnel. There may well be social resistance from the older establishment of politicians and business leaders to the continued increase in salaries, fees, prestige, and influence of the learned professions—even if society as a whole would greatly benefit therefrom.

SCENARIOS FOR CATASTROPHE

Enviornmentalists are often called doomsday prophets by their critics—suggesting that they are compulsive pessimists, predicting inevitable disaster. This is highly misleading. Most environmentalists actually say that disaster is avoidable if present policies are changed, and they are optimistic enough to think that such a change may be possible.

Is it not unduly pessimistic even to raise the possibility

of disaster? Even if shortages and pollution are unavoidable, why should they threaten disaster? The most obvious way, as I have suggested, is by helping to set off World War III through intensified struggles over dwindling supplies of high-quality low-cost resources. (And, as suggested earlier, it would hardly be necessary for all humanity to be killed by direct blast or radiation effects for such a conflict to render the race extinct.) Some environmental catastrophes could also occur without wars—for example, mass poisonings from various pollutants (including dispersed radioactivity), widespread famines, or the raising of temperatures to unlivable heights as a result of waste heat.

Some who admit the potentiality of these dangers may question their inevitability. Why, they may ask, should not growth gradually adapt itself to whatever environmental limits exist—approaching the maximum sustainable level asymptotically, instead of overreaching the limits and then crashing back in traumatic and destructive fashion? Such an orderly approach to limits may well be possible, but under present policies a catastrophic solution is far more likely. For this there are several reasons.

There is first the matter of ignorance. This may be simple ignorance (not knowing) or "advanced ignorance" (knowing what is not so). We are surrounded by dangers of which we know nothing. Even worse, by the dangers that we "know" are not there. For example, in advance of experience, it may be impossible to estimate at what concentration a given pollutant becomes lethal. With respect to thermal pollution, it would be difficult to know how close one was getting to the thermal barrier. And, until recently, we were unaware that a major nuclear exchange would destroy a large part of the ozone layer in the stratosphere that protects all living things from the destructive effects of the ultraviolet rays of the sun. If growth is pushed up to the known limits of safety, it is likely that later knowledge will show that it has exceeded the actual limits of safety.

Even more important then ignorance is the difficulty people have in caring about, or vividly visualizing, the distant future—even their own. Furthermore, as Colin Clark has demonstrated, our economy and motivational system is so structured that rational entrepreneurs will find it in their economic interest to overexploit and destroy even renewable resources, if future income is sufficiently discounted.[17] Essentially, our time-discounting procedures are such that personal maximum profitability now is achieved by destroying the basis for future profitability. For this reason free markets will *not* ensure the conservation of dwindling resources—until the shortages have already become acute.

A third reason is the built-in institutional time lags. According to one major historical school of sociology, "culture lag"—the slowness of religion and tradition-bound behavior to adapt to changes in science and technology—is one of the most fundamental characteristics of every society and the source of much of its internal strain. In the present case, the reluctance to change traditional modes of living despite the shortages and pollution they entail could bring on major tragedy.

A final source of danger arises from the syndrome that has been called "The Tragedy of the Commons."[18] This is a conflict between collective and individual interest, with respect to resources held in common. It is often in the interest of an individual to overuse resources held in common, even though if others act similarly the final effect will be damaging for everybody. The reason why it may still be rational for the individual to act in that way is that even if he abstained, he could not count on others abstaining. Hence, he would lose a short-term advantage anyhow without necessarily averting the final catastrophe.

The standard examples of this syndrome are overgrazing on common pastureland and overfishing in the sea. The same principles apply, however, to overuse of the two common "sinks"—the atmosphere and the sea—as dumps for pollutants, including thermal pollution, and the approach to the thermal barrier. In all these cases, individuals or governments may continue with an ultimately disastrous course of activity because they cannot find a way to subject themselves to restrictions that, if generally enforced, would be in their mutual interest.

For all these reasons, there is no likelihood that a laissez-faire economy will adjust itself smoothly to the environmental built-in limits of what is possible and sustainable. Since we are here concerned almost entirely with what economists call "externalities," it would be impossible for the individual pursuing his own good to end up doing what was best for everyone—as laissez-faire assumes. Beyond this, a satisfactory policy must be based on the best available knowledge and on a very long-run view. Finally, any sacrifices required must be imposed on all alike, lest they be wasted. Clearly, a change in growth policies cannot be spontaneous and individual; it must be planned and implemented by government.

POLICY ALTERNATIVES

To what policies shall we change? Some advocate a continuance of unlimited growth—whatever the possible consequences for our descendants. They argue that if we stop growth we will bring grave evils on ourselves: unemployment, lower living standards, and much government intervention. Our descendants, they say, cannot expect us to ruin our lives to save theirs.

A more subtle variant of this position is the one taken by Herman Kahn of the Hudson Institute. His proposal, in general, is that we should continue unrestricted growth for another 50 or 100 years or so—by which time more people will have achieved affluence and it will be easier to slow down. It is simply a delusion that it would be easier to stop growth in the future than now. True, more people would be affluent, by today's standards, but standards and expectations would have risen sharply; and billions more would be destitute. Meanwhile, the resources for future growth would be seriously depleted.

Essentially, this proposal rationalizes our unwillingness

to face the problem and leaves it to a future generation to make the difficult adjustments for human survival that we are unwilling to make—and to do so under conditions of great deprivation and danger, without even the encouragement of our example.

A STATIONARY STATE

A much more responsible policy, backed by a number of excellent and conscientious economists (the first of whom was John Stuart Mill), would cut the Gordian knot by simply stopping all further growth of population and production. Much as I sympathize with the objectives, I do not find this solution acceptable.

First, it would tend to freeze mankind's material standard of living at much too low a level. The world's per capita GNP in 1973 was only about $1,300, or $25 a week—which means that average personal consumption in most countries was around $15 to $20 a week (or perhaps $18 to $25 at current prices). Obviously, this is not nearly enough to provide the material basis for a good life and freedom from material care. It cannot supply the healthful and enjoyable food, the comfortable and convenient shelter, the highly qualified and motivated educational and health services, nor the privacy, quiet, and dignity of which mankind has always dreamed and that we are now technologically capable of delivering.

To be sure, what we have would go further and would increase the general welfare if it were more equally divided. We must never forget that, according to the World Bank, about one-fifth of the world is living on about $2 a week, in "absolute poverty." But even if wholesale redistribution were possible without loss of capital and income (which I doubt), it would still not change the average. And that average is simply nowhere near enough—as any reader can see by simply trying to imagine living on it. To have to accept it for ourselves and for all future generations would be terribly unfortunate.

My second objection to the stationary state, which may surprise some of its proponents, is that it would not adequately achieve its main objective, that is, to prolong the existence of human civilization. The ultimate recoverable resource of coal (as estimated by the U.S. Geological Survey) would provide only 5,119 years of consumption at existing rates. The comparable figure for iron is 2,657 years; for lead, 162 years; et cetera. The total amounts that could be found might be somewhat greater than this, of course, and additional amounts of some metals might be made available by recycling and substitution—partly at the cost of the additional fuel and metals required for such activities. However, even if we multiply the above figures by some small multiple to take account of such potential supplements and ignore the determination of the developing countries to improve their level of consumption, we are still left with a period of future survival for our civilization that is negligible in relation to man's past 3.5 million years or so on this planet, not to mention his potential future. When planning for the future of human civilization, we should be thinking in terms of millions, not thousands, of years.

Mankind has already grown so large, and its level of consumption so high, that even a freezing of the present situation would not offer mankind an indefinitely prolonged future—and it is precisely *this* that we must seek to ensure.

But are we not being overambitious? Can we ensure mankind an indefinitely prolonged future? Especially, can we do so while raising real living standards? It sounds impossible, and most people believe it is impossible. Yet I believe a solution does exist—which I call dynamic equilibrium.

NOTES

1. David Pimental, L. E. Hurd, A. C. Bellotti, M. J. Forster, I. N. Oka, O. D. Sholes, R. J. Whitman, "Food Production and the Energy Crisis," *Science* 182 (November 2, 1973): 448.

2. Edward J. Mitchell, *U.S. Energy Policy: A Primer* (Washington, D.C.: American Enterprise Institute, 1974).

3. The author is indebted to Robert Triffin, of Yale University, for these estimates.

4. U.S., Atomic Energy Commission, "Reactor Safety Study—An Assessment of Accident Risks in U.S. Commercial Power Plants," WASH-1400, 4 vols. (Washington, D.C.: Atomic Energy Commission, 1975).

5. John T. Edsall, "Hazards of Nuclear Fission Power and the Choice of Alternatives," *Environmental Conservation* 1 (Spring 1974): 21; *idem.* "Further Comments on Hazards of Nuclear Power and the Choice of Alternatives," *Environmental Conservation* 2 no. 8 (Autumn 1975): 205.

6. Carroll Wilson, "A Plan for Energy Independence," *Foreign Affairs* 51 July 1973: 57.

7. William D. Nordhaus, "Resources as a Constraint on Growth," *American Economic Review* 64, no. 2 May 1974: 4.

8. Robert U. Ayres and Allen V. Kneese, "Economic and Ecological Effects of a Stationary State," Reprint no. 99 (Baltimore, Md.: Resources for the Future, December 1972), p. 16. See also Study of Critical Environmental Problems, *Man's Impact on the Global Environment* (Cambridge: Massachusetts Institute of Technology Press, 1970), pp. 63–64; Robert Heilbroner, *An Inquiry into the Human Prospect* (New York: Norton, 1974), pp. 50–55; Nordhaus, "Resources as a Constraint," p. 26.

9. D. H. Meadows, D. L. Meadows, J. Randers, W. W. Behrens III, *The Limits to Growth* (New York: Universe Books, 1972), table 4, pp. 56–60.

10. Nordhaus, "Resources as a Constraint," p. 23.

11. Meadows et al., *Limits to Growth*.

12. *Report on the Limits to Growth.* A study by a Special Task Force of the World Bank (September 1972), p. 43.

13. Nordhaus, "Resources as a Constraint," table 2, p. 24.

14. David B. Brooks and P. W. Anderson, "Mineral Resources, Economic Growth and World Population," *Science* 185 (July 1974): 13.

15. John Brunner, *The Sheep Look Up* (New York: Ballantine, 1973).

16. Carl Kaysen, "The Computer That Printed Out W*O*L*F," *Foreign Affairs* 50 (July 1972): 664.

17. Colin W. Clark, "The Economics of Overexploitation," *Science* 181 (August 1973): 630–34.

18. Garrett Hardin, "The Tragedy of the Commons," *Science* 162 (December 1968): 1243–48.

4

Dynamic equilibrium and survivalism

Through a policy of dynamic equilibrium, humanity may escape the apparent conflict between rising living standards and ecological stability. It is dynamic in that it assumes a continued rapid growth of science, technology, real living standards, and human welfare. But the equilibrium involved is not like a conventional economic equilibrium, where a stable relationship among economic variables is automatically maintained or restored by the free market. This particular equilibrium is between the economy as a whole and the natural environment. It is maintained not automatically but by deliberate policy. And it consists essentially of a balance between the economy and the environment such that the economy may be sustained by the environment far into the indefinite future.

DYNAMIC EQUILIBRIUM

So much for the concept of dynamic equilibrium. How could it be implemented? Essentially, by means of three major policy innovations. Admittedly, at first they appear unacceptable. But they are worth considering carefully—for conditions may later arise that will make acceptable much that is now unacceptable.

The first of these three policies essential for dynamic equilibrium I call conservation/simplification. It involves reducing consumption of nonessential goods made from nonreplenishable resources or made by producing pollution. The most obvious subcategory is sheer waste: the leaky gas lines or steam pipes not repaired; the oversized, uninsulated housing; the factory or public utility discarding its waste heat into a nearby stream or lake, instead of using it to heat a cluster of nearby houses; office buildings so constructed as to require excessive heating in winter and excessive air conditioning in summer; the substitution of high-energy-consuming trucks for trains in long-distance freight hauling; et cetera.

More important, though also more controversial, is the elimination of status-display consumption. Obviously, much of our consumption does not merely assuage our hunger, keep us warm, transport us to where we need to go, and provide other such intrinsic satisfactions. It also displays to others (and to ourselves) that we belong in a socioeconomic group that can afford a certain quantity and quality of consumption. Actually, in our culture we have so muddled intrinsic and extrinsic status-display satisfactions that it is difficult to distinguish between them. As Thorstein Veblen once noted, the shine on a man's sleeve is aesthetically identical with the shine on his shoes, yet one seems attractive and the other not because of their different connotations with respect to affluence.

In other cultures the distinction is easier to see. The Kwakiutl Indians of Canada were accustomed in the potlatch ceremony to burn blankets and canoes in order to establish and exhibit their social status. There was no pretense that this was done to keep warm. The satisfactions were clearly extrinsic. In our own culture we are less explicit. We simply consume items that are bigger, more costly, more expensive to maintain, and more frequently replaced than they need to be.

Thus, we build large and expensive villas many miles from where we work and then hurtle two tons of steel across the landscape daily getting one person back and forth to work. Sheer transportation could as well be supplied by trains, buses, subcompacts, carpools, motorcycles, bicycles, mopeds, et cetera. Ultimately, we would even seek to relocate people so that they could walk to work or take a short trolley ride. Obviously, vested interests stand in the way and have convinced most consumers—largely through endlessly repeated advertising messages—that these things are necessary for a high standard of living.

In criticizing conspicuous consumption, I am not denying the importance of status differentiation and status display. (It seems to be found in all societies—not excepting those formed by egalitarian revolutions.) I merely assert that this could be done in a less wasteful way—for example, by awarding honors, prizes, titles, honorary degrees, special privileges, listings in Who's Whos and social registers, medals, citations, and other nonmonetary rewards. We could, if we wished, allow people who make especially valued contributions to remain rich (even publishing the top section of all income tax returns to facilitate public admiration of the big earners). But we could tax away much of what was not reinvested, so that not even the rich could afford to display their high status by luxury consumption without drawing unfriendly attention from the Internal Revenue Service.

Besides a spendings tax, we would need heavy fines for negligent waste, and close supervision of advertising, restricting it to the sole function of informing consumers of genuinely new and improved products made from smaller quantities of scarce materials, offering greater durability or lower operating and maintenance costs, or polluting less, or

facilitating recycling, or meeting genuine and hitherto un-
met needs—for example, in the field of health, education,
and recreation. In addition very heavy excise taxes might be
placed on items of conspicuous consumption such as big
cars, and public subsidies might be used to help develop
"utility models" of clothing, furniture, housing, cars, et
cetera, aimed at minimum resource consumption, minimum pollution, operating and maintenance costs, and maximum durability and recycling potential. Finally, nonreplenishable raw materials that threaten to be in short supply in
the distant future should be heavily taxed (and if need be,
rationed), with government maintenance of production
through purchase for stockpiling.

To make buying and using goods a less central concern
in our lives, we should put more emphasis on leisure and on
activities. There should be a more rapid reduction in the
workweek, more part-time jobs, and the extension of sab-
baticals to all workers. We should stimulate more individual
participation in sports, intellectual, and esthetic activities
and the arts—for instance, through subsidized competitions
and prizes in athletic contests, chess tournaments, science
fairs and conferences, amateur artistic exhibitions and per-
formances, and outstanding civic contributions.

But would not reductions in waste and in unnecessary
consumption create unemployment? Not necessarily. Essentially, if we have a workable full-employment policy, persons
who stop producing certain unnecessary items would have a
chance to shift to the production of more essential ones—
particularly in reviving industries such as railroads or in
expanding new ones such as the production of methanol and
other new forms of energy and of pollution-control equipment. Moreover, as we shall see, dynamic equilibrium will
produce a shrinking labor force and slow down the introduction of labor-saving machinery—creating a need for labor to
replace retiring personnel. Finally, the new emphasis on
leisure should make for shorter hours, creating additional
work opportunities.

Conservation does imply that consumer sovereignty (of

the present generation of consumers) is not absolute and that some of the things we want—or have been conditioned to want by manipulatory advertising—we just cannot have without imperiling our own and our children's future. Such advertising, if in conflict with conservation's objectives, would have to be stopped. If resources are limited, it makes no sense to create, by psychological manipulation, new material wants, and built-in obsolescence, whether technological or stylistic, would have to be severely curtailed.

Finally, conservation would introduce a new concept of economic productivity. Up to now, productivity gains have involved reducing the amount of labor input (or in some cases, labor and capital input) per unit of output. The new productivity concept introduced by conservation would be measured by the amount of environmental deterioration (depletion of nonrenewable energy and other resources plus pollution produced) per unit of increased output. Perhaps it should be called environmental productivity, which would provide an important supplement to the traditional concept of productivity. In many cases labor-saving machinery and other productivity improvements (in the old sense) would then appear uneconomic—once all the external diseconomies included in the new productivity concept are taken into consideration.

But how can cutting out waste and conspicuous consumption actually raise living standards? The resources saved could, in part, be shifted toward more intrinsically rewarding consumption, and the shift toward increased leisure and more enjoyable activities could enhance real welfare. (A shift of this sort would be of help even in developing countries, especially with respect to their aspirations. It could, for the first time, make developmental aspirations consistent with environmental goals.)

I have argued above that technology would provide no miraculous escape hatch enabling us to escape the limits on growth. I trust I am not being inconsistent here in arguing that only by making the utmost and most effective use of science and technology will it be possible to attain the kind and extent of growth that is achievable and to escape unnecessarily adverse effects from this growth.

I do not share the prejudice of many other environmentalists who blame technology for environmental deterioration. Technology can serve any purpose. How it is used is determined by those who control it (namely, governments and corporations), not by those who create it. So far, technology has served the policy of unrestricted growth, because that was the policy that governments and companies were pursuing. If that policy were ever changed, then the objectives and priorities of science and technology would also be changed, and the whole enterprise would have different results.

The science and technology renewal proposed here would have two aspects. The first part would involve a vast effort to build up our scientific and technological resources to the maximum. Such an effort would be justified by two considerations. The first is that understanding the universe is one of mankind's most exciting and worthwhile activities (indeed, in my own philosophy it is mankind's chief purpose and justification). Second, investment in science and technology has a far larger economic return than investment in anything else. But this cannot be measured in the usual way. First of all, the payoff times are extremely long. Second, the payoffs are often extremely indirect. Thus, there is no real way to trace out and measure the benefits that have been achieved.

All that we can say is that a large part of our modern civilization—television, international communications satellites, antibiotics, jet aircraft, high fidelity, computers, calculators, et cetera—is the result of a few dozen billion dollars, at the most, of investment in R&D. If their current and future contribution to human welfare could be expressed in dollars, it would be an enormous multiple of that investment. There is simply no other kind of investment that is remotely as productive. (To be sure, this investment has also created nuclear weapons. But the governments directing these particular R&D programs were, after all, trying to develop weapons, and no one can deny that, as weapons, these were an unqualified success. The fact that having a lot of extremely potent weapons around may reduce our security is no argument against the efficacy of R&D in achieving the various objectives for which it has been used.)

At this stage, then, our aim should be to spend as much as possible on science and technology. The restraints should *never* be merely budgetary but should arise solely from the limitations imposed by the absence of qualified people and lack of worthwhile projects. Such needs may, moreover, be substantially reduced, if we are willing to spend the money required to develop the right sort of people. Many talented young people either receive no higher education at all or train for other professions because future opportunities in science and technology appear uncertain or inadequate. (This is inevitable when we cut back in real support for R&D and higher education and allow significant unemployment to develop among scientists and engineers. Such policies are completely irresponsible.)

Beyond this, there must be many thousands of children in the developing countries who have enormous scientific potential but whose poverty bars them from any chance of even elementary, let alone advanced, education. From any one of these children, if he or she were properly trained, might ultimately spring an idea as fundamental as the quantum theory or a technology as prolific as the computer. If we only had the vision, we would realize that it would be worth supporting and training and ultimately giving R&D jobs to thousands and thousands of such children for the benefits we might obtain from the ideas developed by a single one of them. This is one kind of foreign aid from which everyone would benefit.

The second part of the renewal of science and technology would involve a major shift in priorities. So far, the vast bulk of our R&D effort has been in weapons improvement, in the discovery and utilization of fossil and nuclear fuels, in transport and communication, in productivity improvements in the old sense (usually of reducing labor inputs per unit of output), and in consumer trivia (car styling, convenience packaging, marketing techniques, et cetera).

The new priorities we now need, to serve the goals of dynamic equilibrium, would emphasize energy and materials conservation and the development of new nonpolluting energy and materials (especially solar energy) and of productivity improvements (especially in the new sense of using less-scarce energy and materials, providing maximum durability with minimum repairs and servicing and facilitating recycling). Some examples of these new priorities would be: biological controls over insect pests and predators; use of garbage to produce methanol; use of feed-lot manure to produce valuable protein for animal foodstuffs; final steps in the development of new low-gas-consumption and low-pollution engines; and elaborate research in pollution to improve our ability to detect it, to evaluate its danger, and to prevent, dissipate, or neutralize it.

Essentially, then, science and technology renewal would help us to achieve the highest living standards compatible with minimal environmental pollution and depletion and would reduce, ultimately, environmental damage to minimal proportions. It would help enable us to maintain and raise these living standards without the unemployment and inflation we experience now.

But how could such vast new government programs be financed without inflation? Mainly, by revenues from the spendings tax and the taxes on scarce commodities and polluting processes. Partly, by royalties from government-owned patents and publications. But also by savings on transfer payments to the poor (such as welfare payments, food stamps, and unemployment insurance), since the amounts of these would be greatly diminished as the result of the third part of the dynamic equilibrium program, to which we now turn.

The most radical and controversial, but perhaps also the most fundamental, part of the dynamic equilibrium program is negative population growth (NPG)—deliberate reduction of population size by reducing the birthrate, instead of waiting until there is an unavoidable increase in the death rate.

There are indications that most countries have populations that are much larger than optimum and that they could substantially increase their per capita incomes simply by reducing the number of people. Studies of developing countries have strongly indicated that reductions in population growth might be many times as effective (perhaps 100 times as effective) as traditional development programs in raising per capita incomes.[1] My preliminary study of 140 developing countries (with under $1,000 per capita income) showed a decisive negative correlation of −0.2783 between population growth and growth of per capita income—significant at better than a 1 percent confidence level.* Multiple regression with a smaller sample and for an earlier period also showed a significant negative correlation. For a group of developed countries, there was also a negative correlation, but it was not strong enough to be significant. Such studies do not rigorously demonstrate a causal connection, or the direction of causation if a causal bond does exist, but they do at least suggest that a reduction in the rate of population growth would help to increase per capita income.

The essential mechanism that would bring this about is not hard to visualize. The reduction in new births is likely to promote an increase in savings and an increase in investment relative to consumption. More important, it is likely to promote a shift in type of investment—with less emphasis on housing, sewerage, clearing new lands, et cetera, which are necessary to keep up with a rising population; and with more emphasis on investment in machinery and equipment, advanced education and technical training, et cetera, which will be required to raise productivity and output. In general

---

*The correlation factor is −0.2783, significant at better than a 1 percent level. Multiple regression with a smaller sample and for an earlier period also showed a significant negative correlation. [The study referred to was published as Emile Benoit, *Defense and Economic Growth in Developing Countries* (Lexington, Mass.: Heath, 1973).]—Editor's note.

productivity would benefit from improved man/land and man/capital ratios; and the offsetting loss from the slower growth in the labor force would be relatively small where there was already substantial unemployment and underemployment. Note that even if NPG were associated with a smaller or negative growth in output, there might still be a more rapid increase in per capita incomes because of the smaller number of people among whom the income was divided.

Some individuals who accept that slower population growth would raise per capita incomes are reluctant to accept the further conclusion that reductions in population might also raise per capita incomes. They buttress their reluctance with a variety of arguments that I find quite unconvincing. They fear, for instance, that the violent change in age composition would after a time result in an increased number of dependents relative to the size of the working population.[2] But the increased share of retired persons when NPG went into effect would be balanced off by the decrease in the number of children and—what has not been taken into account—by the increased number of women entering into paid employment, or full-time self-employment, as a result of much smaller families. Further increases in the labor force, if desired, could be obtained by raising the age of retirement and providing more and better child care programs to permit more mothers of young children to work. In any case such age composition adjustments would be of a temporary character and could not remotely offset the basic benefits of an improved man/land and man/capital ratio, the elimination of unemployment and underemployment, and the diversion of investment away from housing and other population-related uses into machines, technical education, and other productivity-enhancing uses.

In the developed countries, the benefits of NPG for raising per capita GNP are more controversial, but NPG is strongly advisable in any case in order to permit increases in average living standards while reducing consumption of nonreplaceable raw materials and the creation of pollution. In addition the developed countries must lead the way, or else the developing countries will tend to regard the advocacy of NPG as inspired by genocidal motives.

To be sure, population reduction is not one of those good things of which one can say "the more of it the better": a high per capita income with no "capita" would be a *reductio ad absurdum*. Up to a certain point, however, NPG does promise large benefits. We urgently need research to help us determine where the point is beyond which the adverse effects of a decline in the labor force outbalance the benefits of having fewer consumers competing for the available supplies.

If we go beyond mere income maximization, and include environmental considerations, the argument is further strengthened. Population reduction would necessarily reduce the amount of energy and raw materials that had to be used to produce a given standard of living and would reduce the amount of pollution with which it would be accompanied. Thus, if we consider externalities, NPG will almost inevitably be beneficial.

Aside from its possible merits, NPG seems to most people utterly unrealistic. The idea of built-in inevitable population growth seems to be part of the natural order of things. We forget that for most of the 3.5 million years that mankind has inhabited this earth his numbers grew very slowly and occasionally declined. And we overlook the enormous potential significance of the new technology for separating sexuality from procreation.

NPG will be the most difficult of the three policies to implement. It requires two separate things: first, effective, convenient, inexpensive and available contraceptives; and, second, the creation of adequate motivation for their use to the point where the average number of children per family falls substantially below the number presently desired. (The number of surviving children will of course fall below the number of children born.) Both the technological and the motivational aspects of the problem pose grave difficulties.

The first step may be to convince governments that large populations no longer provide greater military strength or world influence but constitute a major drag on the progress and modernization they seek, as well as a threat to their own and the world's future. Most governments still have essentially pronatalist policies, originally adopted when populations were small and fertile land abundant. They give people tax advantages if they are married and in proportion to the number of their dependent children. Relief payments, family allowances, and other social benefits are generally in proportion to the number of children. Children are given free or subsidized education, regardless of the number of children in the family. Moreover, parents—especially in rural areas—are allowed to profit substantially from the labor of their children, thereby greatly strengthening the incentive to have more of them. On top of all this, most countries restrict, in various degrees, access to birth control and abortion services—or at least fail to encourage their effective use. None of them has even adopted the simple expedient of paying people special allowances and pensions if they have no more than one or two children.

The more fundamental measure, however, to facilitate NPG would be to create new forms of contraception that are free, convenient, effective, without possible adverse health effects, and usable under primitive hygienic conditions. Something like this, involving annual injections, may soon be available.[3] Most people in developing countries are by now accustomed to injections to combat disease, and resistance to such methods would presumably be low—especially if accompanied by regular cash payments.

To maximize per capita GNP, population would have to be reduced only to the point where labor shortages did not outbalance the benefits of having fewer consumers to share the GNP and the chance to divert more savings into productivity-enhancing types of investment. However, to maximize long-term welfare, it might be desirable to reduce population somewhat more than this, in order to minimize adverse environmental effect—especially if the reduction in per capita GNP were concentrated in wasteful and consumption items with small intrinsic contributions to welfare.

I am convinced that if mankind's numbers were sufficiently reduced, if its technical advancement were sufficiently rapid and sufficiently devoted to the solution of environmental problems, and if there were proper conservation of energy and scarce materials, a situation could be reached in which mankind and its material culture would be truly in equilibrium with the natural environment and could continue without endangering the viability of future generations.

SURVIVALISM

Who is to make these policy changes? Assuredly, they will not happen of their own accord. I look to a broad-based movement, comprised of many groups and dedicated to bringing about dynamic equilibrium and allied policies. The strongest support for such a movement should come initially from the scientific community, a community that is professionally involved in discovering and publicizing the truth. Support and help should come from other important related groups: conservationists, environmentalists, population and arms control advocates, and liberal religious groups that feel unashamed of overt idealism. The confederation of these groups I would call the Survivalist movement. United in this way, it could create a climate of opinion that would be ultimately irresistible.

Where would it start? Clearly, at this stage the emphasis must be on education and publicity. The prime objective is to get the message of survivalism to as many people as possible, making use of whatever help is available from likeminded groups—while at the same time getting these groups to recognize their convergent interest in human survival as a necessary precondition of their separate goals and to recognize the benefits of a more active type of mutual cooperation.

In order to maintain public visibility, and more important, to get us through the short term that must precede the long term on which Survivalists must keep their eyes fixed, Survivalists must involve themselves in solving current controversial problems that have long-term implications for human survival, which have generally been neglected. By getting involved in such discussions, Survivalists should call themselves to the public's attention, identify themselves as the present-day champions of humankind's long-term interests, and continue to hammer away at the basic, though usually ignored, point: Wherever possible we should seek solutions to short-term problems, which will make it easier, rather than harder, to find solutions to the more fundamental and difficult long-term problems.

Let us now consider three such problems and the positions that Survivalists might adopt with respect to them.

INFLATIONARY RECESSION

The most urgent and widely deplored economic problem of our day is the combination of rapid inflation and serious unemployment. Most economists initially found it unbelievable and still find it inexplicable. It is sometimes now called "stagflation," but this is misleading. Production has not merely stagnated; it has declined. U.S. industrial production in the last quarter of 1975 was about 9 percent below the level reached two years earlier. Yet this decline has been accompanied by an extraordinary bout of inflation.

There is good reason for survivalists to be concerned. It must be remembered that the European inflation of the 1920s, which was followed by the world depression of the 1930s, set the stage for World War II. Today the stakes have, of course, been upped considerably. Thus, Survivalists should insist that a restoration of the status quo ante is not sufficient, since that condition was unstable and unviable. In particular Survivalists should support recovery methods that would also help the economy to cope with the long-term dangers it confronts.

But is this not a counsel of perfection? Do we even know how to restore full employment and stop inflation? I strongly believe so. The best-developed part of the solution is with respect to full-employment policy. Here, I think all the important substantive problems—and most of the procedural ones as well—have been satisfactorily solved by John H. G. Pierson.[4] Pierson calls for full, not merely "maximum," employment: real jobs for all who want them and are able to do them—setting aside only a small margin of truly unavoidable frictional unemployment. Full employment should be guaranteed by definite government commitments. The guarantee feature, by stabilizing expectations, would contribute greatly (like a self-fulfilling prophecy) to achieving the goal. It would help avoid the perpetual swings between excessive and deficient rates of investment and consumption, with excessive wage pressure and price boosts in periods of recovery and boom.

What sort of government commitments would be required? First, an underwriting of the necessary rate of consumer spending, which together with the government's own planned expenditure and the anticipated associated amount of investment and foreign trade would create the targeted number of jobs. Second, a subsidiary government guarantee to supply additional useful short-term public jobs to the extent that *despite* the adequacy of consumer spending there was nevertheless an unanticipated shortfall of jobs. The second guarantee (of government "last resort" employment) would never be acceptable in a private enterprise system without the first (an ensured adequate level of consumer spending).

Maintenance of consumer expenditure could be guaranteed by institution of "highly flexible" withholding taxes that could readily be reduced (or flexible transfer payments that could be increased) to whatever extent necessary whenever consumer spending began to run short of the level underwritten. All this differs somewhat from "fine tuning"—with its gross risks of oversteering. Government intervention should not depend on forecasts, which have often proved unreliable, but upon observed indexes of actual performance. Moreover, Congress should periodically set employment and purchasing power goals and provide the administration (either exclusively or through a mixed congressional-executive committee) with strong discretionary tools, particularly the power (under certain agreed conditions) to make frequent and substantial changes in tax withholding rates within predetermined limits and to expand or contract employment on already approved and authorized public projects. (Lacking such tools, past efforts to maintain full employment inevitably failed.)

Incidentally, such solutions to the unemployment problem do not require that the public sector be any larger than the electorate desires for its own sake. Government is replete with redundant jobs intended primarily to reward partisan political services and contributions. Any additional government bureaucracy required by such proposals could be easily offset by the reduction in patronage jobs. More important, many jobs in antipoverty agencies would be rendered unnecessary by the elimination of mass poverty through full employment.

How can this be combined with inflation control? Here we are on more controversial ground. Nevertheless, I have recently put forward a proposal, which some people think useful. (It is really too specialized to explain in this part of the book; those interested may turn to the "Excursus on the Inflation/Unemployment Trade-off'" at the end of the chapter.) But let me cite one point from the proposal that particularly illustrates the survivalist approach to such problems. I begin with the observation that deficit-financed tax cuts are virtually the whole of the present government's recovery program. Such tax cuts are now widely approved by economists for this purpose, and I have myself been arguing in their favor for 30 years.[5]

Nevertheless, today, speaking as a Survivalist, I must

deplore such an exaggerated dependence on this particular policy tool. For even if effective in stimulating a higher level of activity, deficit-financed tax cuts merely restore the pattern of consumption, production, and employment that existed before the recession began. They do nothing to change that pattern in a way that would reduce pollution and depletion of scarce resources. Actually, with recovered affluence and an enlarged population, one would expect that the adverse environmental impacts would be worse than ever.

The change we need is a change along lines conducive to survival. Such changes can be promoted, and the economy stimulated, by government subsidies or contracts to revive certain old industries and to develop certain new ones that will be helpful in meeting the basic environmental challenges that confront us. The most crucial of these industries are higher education and the training of R&D capabilities. Other old industries that need revival are the railroads and the streetcars, which under the onslaught of the politically powerful highway lobby have been allowed to fall to pieces or have been otherwise destroyed. This has occurred despite the fact that at any moment our oil imports might be discontinued and part of our oil supply diverted to support our allies. Railroad transportation is in any case vastly more economical and less polluting. There is also much to be done in the renovation and modernization of structurally sound housing that is now rapidly deteriorating—if not already deserted.

An example of a new industry that should be quickly expanded is the production of methanol, or wood alcohol, which can be distilled from garbage and other organic wastes. A mixture of gasoline and up to 15 percent of methanol will run in ordinary gasoline engines at lower temperatures, with less pollution and only slight sacrifice of mileage, at a substantial economy. Another new industry deserving stimulation is the development of a low-emission and fuel-efficient engine.[6] Still others are new techniques for pollution monitoring, assessment, and abatement; the development of other energy substitutes (particularly the various forms of solar energy); and mass production of motorbikes, mopeds, bicycles, et cetera.

The usual answer to such proposals is that the government cannot afford such large programs. There is an element of sheer self-deception in such an answer. The fact is that by 1975 the federal expenditure on goods and services was 22 percent less than it had been in 1968 in real terms (discounting for increases in the general price level).* Translated into 1976 prices, it would have amounted to $45 billion. In other words, the federal government could now spend over $45 billion more on the purchases of goods and services, and it would still not be taking more actual goods and services away from the rest of the economy than it did in 1968.

If the federal government mounted a new environmental program of anywhere near this size, the recession would quickly be over and full employment quickly restored. What is more important, the basic program required for a dynamic equilibrium economy would be well on its way. But would this not be violently inflationary? Not if it were in substitution for a somewhat larger amount of deficit-financed tax cuts. Deficit-financed government expenditures are slightly more stimulating than deficit-financed tax cuts, and this would have to be taken into consideration in the size of the program. However, any revival program at all will be inflationary in the present context, and this is why a special set of policies is required to handle "inflationary recession." (Once more, I refer the reader to the "Excursus" at the end of the chapter.)

Would the proposed program not make an already oversized government even larger? By no means. First, almost all of the funds would go to private recipients, universities, research establishments, private contractors, or

---

* [The 1978 expenditure for goods and services was over 28 percent less than the 1968 expenditure for goods and services, calculated in constant dollars. Editor's note.]

businesses receiving subsidies to finance environmental projects desired by the government. The small additional number of government employees required to plan, administer, and supervise these projects (and the other operations required to maintain full employment and hold down inflation) could easily be offset by dropping an equal number of make-work and antipoverty jobs, as previously suggested.

THE ENERGY SQUEEZE

The energy squeeze is a topic that is of intense popular interest and a topic in which survivalism has an obvious justification for getting involved. As I have suggested, quarrels with suppliers could easily touch off World War III. And attempts to find a quick substitute for oil imports by a rapid expansion of nuclear power plants pose serious short-term ecological dangers. The alternatives offered by Survivalism are enormously superior.

The most crucial decision for the near term is to determine how much energy we need. This question is often asked but usually asked wrongly. "Requirements" are automatically calculated in terms of past levels of per capita consumption, projected to increase in line with past long-term trends. The problem is then conceived in terms of how much of this total would still be derived from unreliable imports and how much could be replaced by additional domestic production. It is assumed that unless these requirements are met one way or the other, employment and standards of living will decline.

The Survivalist must challenge this whole way of looking at the problem. The fact is that Switzerland and Germany, which have per capita incomes and living standards quite comparable with the United States, nevertheless manage to get along on per capita energy use that is only one-third and one-half, respectively, of what we have in the United States.[7] Of course, the United States is bigger and more spread out, but clearly it could achieve its present standard of living with a lot less energy than it is now using. If in the future it adopts dynamic equilibrium, with the elimination of waste and conspicuous consumption, with the invention of more energy-efficient technologies, and with the reduction of population size, then the amount of energy required could become even much less.

This viewpoint transforms the essential problem. It is no longer How can we find a reliable source of additional energy to meet requirements? Instead it becomes: By what path can we best start cutting back the amount of energy used without damaging real welfare?

When this latter question has been discussed, the three main alternatives considered have been exhortation, price increases, and rationing.

Exhortation is not a satisfactory basis for bringing about needed social changes, for reasons explained by Garrett Hardin in "The Tragedy of the Commons.[8] Those who sacrifice their inclinations out of a sense of public obligation will be taken advantage of by those lacking in public spirit, and it is the latter who will proliferate. Eventually, those who comply will be praised, but at present they will actually be viewed, even by the government, with contempt. Thus, the attitude of a survivalist should be: I shall waste as much as my neighbor, if it suits my convenience, while working hard to pass laws that will prevent either of us from committing serious waste.

Price increases are more effective but are not the definitive and exclusively appropriate solution supposed by many economists. Are price increases necessary to provide higher profits to the producers to enable them to find and develop new energy sources? Probably not, and particularly if we do not *need* new and additional energy supplies but do need to cut back consumption. Yet even for this purpose, are not price increases just what are needed? In some cases, yes—as in the use of gas for industrial power, or even for home heating. Unfortunately, it turns out that the demand for gasoline for automobiles is rather inelastic (that is, the amount bought does not change much when the price changes). At least this is true in the short and medium run.

To cut consumption decisively, prices would have to be raised to extremely high levels. Then we would face the difficulty that the sacrifices would be very inequitably shared, since many people now need to use cars to get to work or shopping areas. If price rises for gasoline forced some people to lose their jobs or their homes while richer people could still use their cars for pleasure driving, this would create great disorganization and discontent.

Rationing would distribute the sacrifice more evenly, and by making sacrifice politically tolerable, it would permit a serious effort to start cutting down consumption. In addition it would give an unambiguous signal to car producers and car consumers that large cars should no longer be produced. It is sheer cowardice on the part of our leaders that they have not explained to the public why rationing was needed and have not solicited their support in doing it.

What our leaders have emphasized—and I think exaggerated—is the administrative difficulty in enforcing such a system in peacetime. Assuming that cutting back energy use was recognized as a life and death matter, justifying very heavy penalties on violators and payment of large rewards to informers—and given the availability today of computer technology to help detect infractions—I simply cannot credit that enforcement problems would be insuperable.

No system of blind energy use cutbacks without the provision of substitutes, however, would be economically or politically tolerable. To cut back on long-distance trucking, we would need a revived railraod system with piggyback capabilities. To eliminate the use of large private cars, we would need first to subsidize the production of bicycles, motorcycles, mopeds (perhaps the construction of special paths for them as well), minicars, and subcompacts—not to mention buses, passenger trains, and trolley cars. And to cut back on home-heating fuel, we need not only to adequately subsidize the proper insulation of homes but also to cut off the tax deduction for interest payments on mortgages and to provide comparable tax advantages for apartment houses.

Until we reorganize our living arrangements, and live near where we work, shop, and go to school, we shall still need a great deal of transportation. We cannot stop or curtail the use of our existing transport mechanisms— however energy inefficient they may be—until we can provide substitutes.

It is precisely now—when we have a major recession with millions out of work and excess capacity in many industries—that we have a chance to build the new low-energy technology that we will need for the time ahead. The Survivalist message is: Solve the energy squeeze in a way that will make us less vulnerable to an oil squeeze in the future *and* that will leave more useful energy for our descendants. Try to learn from it what changes are necessary.

WORLD HUNGER

The third topic of immediate concern in Survivalism is world hunger. This topic raises difficult ethical as well as public policy questions. Hunger, true hunger—*serious* long-continued undernourishment—is probably the source of more human misery than anything else in the world. The problem is getting worse all the time. Hunger is actually a sort of dull torture that in time destroys bodies and spirits and over time prevents human beings from developing properly. This condition may affect some 10 to 20 percent of the world's population. A good number of the deaths attributed to various diseases is actually due to weakened resistance owing to undernutrition. Furthermore, the number of people dying from actual famine is on the increase and seems likely to get worse. What, if anything, can be done about it? What guidance, if any, can Survivalism offer?

There are essentially three approaches to a solution.

The first, which I call the technological approach, involves continuing to increase food production. The second approach, which I call the redistributionist approach, involves shifting food away from excessive or luxury consumption over to those who are hungry. The third approach, which I call the ecological approach, involves limiting the number of people, so that there is more food per person and more resources remain unused, in the hope that future generations will not have to go hungry either. Almost all public attention is focused on the first two approaches—raising more food or redistributing it.

In the previous chapter, I explained the overwhelming difficulties in increasing food output at all rapidly, especially in an age of energy and capital shortages, soil erosion, and likely adverse climatic developments. If, despite our best efforts, we are left with nearly a billion people who are hungry, and many millions who are actually starving, redistribution would seem to be the only remaining solution.

Concerning the redistributionist approach, we must first remind ourselves that the international aid that has been given so far, including food aid, has apparently reduced hunger little if at all. The United States alone has given $14 billion in official food aid to poor countries over the years, and other countries have also contributed. Vastly larger sums were given in general developmental aid, which saved foreign exchange but which could have been used for additional food imports or imports to improve agricultural productivity. And, of course, there is a considerable volume of private charity. Yet there are now more hungry people than ever.

Why has all this not accomplished more? For years most of the developing countries have had available the technology and the resources for building up agricultural output. But they have done little to set up the field services to transfer this technology to the marginal farmers or to establish the cooperatives to help them finance the new production and to store and market the increased output. Why?

Basically, because the governments of most of the poor countries have set quite a low priority on relieving the hunger of their subjects. Most of the foreign aid has been used for strengthening the political and financial positions of the existing leaders, for military buildups, and for industrialization. What is spent on agriculture is mainly on large-scale agriculture with export-or import-substitution potentials. In the end very little of it gets to the hungry.

On the basis of past experience, it therefore seems quite unlikely that a continuation or increase of foreign aid along traditional lines will reduce the number of hungry people. Indeed, the U.S. State Department projects that the gap between grain production and requirements will more than triple in the developing countries over the next decade—even assuming a continuation of food aid.

As the real costs of producing food have risen, resistance to increases in traditional food aid has also increased. As reserve stocks in the donor nations have been exhausted, a major crop failure would bring risks of hunger even in rich nations. Moreover, under present conditions exportable food surpluses are highly salable items that producers count on to finance the enormously expanded cost of oil imports.

A policy that increases the number of half-starving people in the world by keeping some of them from actually starving to death would, in any case, not be a particularly inspiring one from an ethical viewpoint—even if it worked. What we really need, by contrast, is a way of reducing the number of people who die of hunger *and* who suffer from hunger. To find a way, we will have to include a large element of the ecological approach.

Ecologists premise a natural relationship between the number of members of any species and the environment, a relationship that holds that number within fairly constant parameters. During most of the 3 million years that *Homo sapiens* has been around, his numbers were kept down to the required levels by predators, diseases, and, occasionally, scarcity of game. But man frequently also practiced primitive forms of contraception and abortion and practiced infanticide quite widely.

This situation changed quite dramatically around 10,000 to 15,000 years ago because of the agricultural revolution, which suddenly expanded man's food supply by a large multiple. Suddenly, there seemed no ecological need to control numbers. In fact since settled habitations were required for agriculture, and large populations were helpful in defending such habitations against marauders, there was every reason to encourage the largest possible populations. The new religions arising in agricultural societies rationalized this situation and instructed their disciples to "go forth and multiply."

Ideologically, we are still living in this era. In reality the new ecological niche created by the agricultural revolution has now been fully exploited, and our population is again at the point where various built-in controls are taking over. Death rates are again beginning to rise from malnutrition, and millions are tortured and enfeebled by hunger.

Earlier in the chapter, I suggested that population control is the most effective means for raising per capita incomes. Likewise, it would be particularly helpful in eliminating hunger, since it is among subsistence farmers (and their progeny that migrate to city slums) that underemployment and hunger are worst.

How can we combine this insight with our own powerful ethical impulses that force us to do something *now* to help those who are already hungry or already facing starvation? My own proposed solution, which seems to me to be in line with the Survivalist approach, is as follows.

The developed countries should establish a new international agency, presumably associated with the United Nations, in which control would remain primarily in the hands of the donor countries, as for example in the International Monetary Fund or the World Bank. Most or all of the world's bilateral food aid and perhaps other economic aid would be distributed through this agency. The agency would be committed to distributing such aid not primarily on the basis of development opportunities, conventionally conceived, but on the basis of the willingness and the cooperation shown by the recipient governments in establishing effective systems for reducing birthrates—by establishing birth control and abortion services and motivating people to use them.

The last point is crucial, because, unfortunately, most leaders and development planners of developing countries do not conceive of population controls as development programs. Faced with a choice between obtaining a cement plant or getting a program to transform the nation's midwives into a paramedical corps and family-planning auxiliary, they would almost invariably choose the cement plant as a part of their development program, assuming that family planning was a contribution only to public health and welfare. If they had a broader view of the realities, they might perceive that the midwife program if truly effective could conceivably add a lot more to future per capita GNP than the cement plant and should be regarded as a particularly high-powered development project. I have already suggested the outlines of effective population control programs: better contraceptives, a revision of pension policies to reward those who have few children and penalize those who have many, and other incentive programs.

The moral and religious objections of individuals to family limitation may ultimately place a major limitation on further progress in reducing family size, but we are not yet at that stage. There are still apparently many millions of unwanted births, and a surprisingly large number of these occur in families already practicing contraception. We know, moreover, that some Catholic countries have a far lower birthrate than others and that Catholics (and others whose faiths or ideologies officially object to birth control) patronize family-planning clinics in nearly the same ratio to their numbers as do other groups in the population. Thus, considerable progress would still appear possible in reducing unwanted births; while we reduce the numbers of these, some of the ideological objections to family limitation may weaken.

The basic rationale of tying up aid receipts of developing countries with effective population control is that if—ecologically speaking—there are too many people, then there has to be either a rise in the death rate or a decline in the birthrate. International donations are bound to be limited, even if the donors are increasingly generous. The best use for the available aid is, therefore, to keep alive and make more productive those who are seriously trying to reduce population. To help those who will continue with rapid population growth is to help increase the number of hungry people who will require more help—ad infinitum. To give the available help to those who will create the least need for additional help is to maximize the benefits achieved per dollar of aid given.

This avoids, or at least softens, some of the ethical dilemmas associated with so-called triage, which puts upon the donor the responsibility for deciding who shall receive help and who shall not. The method proposed here would allow the decision to be made by an international agency and in the last analysis by the recipient countries. Those who prefer to have their populations reduced by a large increase in the death rate would be free to do so. Those who prefer to control their populations by a decline in the birthrate would be helped to achieve it in that way.

Even so, some recipient nations will no doubt regard this as imposed population control, even though they would be perfectly free to turn down the foreign aid offered on this basis, and would level accusations of genocide. The only way to get around this is for the donor countries to accept the same population control programs and objectives that the international aid organization is requiring aid recipients to adopt.

For this there is good inherent justification, from a survivalist viewpoint. While the populations of the developing countries are growing much more slowly, their per capita contribution to pollution and to depletion of scarce resources is much larger. Thus, even if they have few hungry people and high average consumption, they, too, would benefit themselves and the world by NPG. Only when programs to achieve this have been adopted in the developed countries can we expect the developing countries to regard such programs without a degree of distrust.

But are aid funds sufficient to finance such programs? Clearly, yes, if they are taken out of the present foreign aid funds for all purposes. At present the part of foreign aid devoted to population control assistance is ludicrously small. Most countries devote less than 1 percent of their bilateral aid to population projects, and even the United States has given only about $60 million a year for it in recent years. The UN Fund for Population Activities approved only $68 million in 1974 and was promised only $90 million in 1976. It has had to reject about half of the requests received because of lack of funds.[9] (Not to give the developing countries all the technical assistance they want in controlling their populations is, from a Survivalist viewpoint, utter insanity.)

To sum up, then, the Survivalist contribution to the world hunger discussion is to point out that increasing production has not solved the problem, and will not. Redistribution, in the sense of traditional foreign aid, also cannot solve the problem—if only because the recipient governments will insist on using most of it for other purposes. The only way even partially to solve the problem is to channel most foreign aid into an international agency, controlled by the aid donors, which will use most of its funds to help the recipients achieve NPG, and which will allocate its remaining aid only for agricultural programs and to countries that participate actively and successfully in the population program. Moreover, the donor countries must adopt similar NPG programs to remove any stigma from them.

Less aid would then be available for conventional development programs. This would probably mean that development would proceed faster. As previously noted, a given sum of money spent on population controls would raise the per capita GNP up to 100 times as fast as the same amount spent on conventional development programs. And with fewer public funds for investment in industry, there would be more reliance on private investment, where the level of productivity tends to be much higher.

And if the international aid agency would spend money only for population and agricultural programs and would insist on close control of how funds were spent—with immediate cutoffs if suspicion of diversion arose—then perhaps this program could genuinely do something at last to put an end to the torture of world hunger.

Here is a case where, despite surface appearances, the humanitarian goal of stopping human suffering and the Survivalist goal of safeguarding man's future overlap rather neatly. By advocating policies that make sense on both levels, Survivalists can render a double service.

INTERNATIONAL INEQUALITY

At present the 25 percent of the world's population living in developed countries that create 79 percent of the world's GNP* is absorbing the bulk of the world's raw materials and creating the bulk of the world's pollution. This is profoundly inequitable. But it is widely believed and frequently repeated that the vast inequalities between the poor and the rich nations create one of the world's most serious and urgent problems and that the failure to reduce the international income gap—or even to prevent it from widening further—is a major source of international tension and threat to peace. Survivalists should not accept this belief uncritically. To make a major issue of international inequalities only attracts attention away from these enormously more serious and urgent problems and plays into the hands of those who are not interested in achieving real economic progress but in making political capital out of alleged economic failure.

---

*[Calculated on the basis of the 1976 population and the 1976 GNP. Editor's note.]

What do we mean by *inequality?* The two fundamental forms of inequality among nations are differences in the number of people and differences in their per capita incomes. These differences underlie most of the other inequalities, including the differences in political and military power that may be more directly related to questions of war and peace. Differences in the number of people and in per capita income are not only fundamental but are largely independent of each other. Thus, we have large but poor nations like India and China, small but rich nations like Switzerland and Belgium, large and rich ones like the United States and the United Kingdom or the Soviet Union, and small but poor ones like Dahomey and Togo.

For the sake of simplicity, I shall discuss the income gap on the basis of national differences in per capita GNP, as assembled from standard sources, or estimated, by the Economics Division of the U.S. Arms Control and Disarmament Agency.[10] I am well aware of the technical limitations of this type of estimate, among them that it tends to exaggerate the real differences in living standards between developed and developing nations[11] by making inadequate allowance for the value of self-produced and unmarketed goods and services and for the greater cheapness of living in the developing countries, owing to their generally much lower transportation, heating, and marketing costs.

Even if such estimates do somewhat exaggerate the real income gap, they, nevertheless, suggest that the gap must still be very large. In 1976 the average GNP per capita of the developed countries was estimated at over 11 times as large as the average for the developing countries. People who talk glibly about narrowing this income gap have not, in my view, begun to understand the real nature of the problem.

Recently (from 1964 to 1970) the average per capita growth rate has been 3.2 percent for the developing countries as against 3.7 percent for the developed countries.*

---

* This discrepancy is wholly attributable to the more rapid population growth of the developing countries. On a total GNP basis (that is, not per

Now even if these rates were reversed, the gap would still continue to widen, and rapidly. In fact, if we project such growth rates to the end of this century, we find that in the year 2000 the gap between the developed and the developing countries would still be over twice as great as it is now. Even if we were to make the quite unrealistic assumption that the developing countries could immediately double their 1970 rates, while the developed countries grew at only 3.2 percent per annum, this would hardly change the projection at all. The gap in the year 2000 would still be more than twice what it is now and continuing to widen rapidly.

Even if this reversal could be achieved would the necessary cutting out of nearly 90 percent of the developed countries' present growth rates be worth it? Such rates would spell virtual stagnation and permanent recession in the developed countries; with growth far below achievable productivity gains, there would be steadily rising unemployment and make-work—with grave political effects. Before long the growth of the developing countries would be adversely affected by the shrinking opportunities to export to developed countries and by the falloff of foreign aid and investment—so that even the goal of shrinking the income gap would probably be missed. But the large income gap is going to remain and cannot be changed much one way or the other in the immediate future. So long as it is there, most people will not really care very much whether it is statistically increasing or decreasing. This is a matter of third-rate importance and certainly not worth pursuing if it would require major economic and political disruptions in the developed countries.

What *is* really important is to raise the absolute levels of the poor countries in a tangible way that gives hope for the

---

capita basis), the developing country growth rate exceeded that of the developed countries. [The mean annual rate between 1967 and 1976 was 4.5 percent for developed countries and 2.9 percent for developing countries, a trend that reinforces the author's skepticism about the optimistic hypotheses he considers below and underscores his conclusions. Editor's note.]

future. Income equality seems to me in no way comparable in importance with a goal of eliminating severe poverty. Income inequality achieved or perpetuated by military and political means (that is, colonialism) may be an absolute evil whose eradication deserves a high priority, but this is because of the methods by which the inequalities have been created or maintained, not because inequality in itself is such a serious evil. And allegations that existing international inequalities are mainly attributable to past colonialism are hardly consistent with a number of obvious facts. Thus, some countries or peoples that were never or only briefly colonialized (for example, Thailand, Ethiopia, New Guinea, the Australian aborigines, and the Indians of the upper Amazon) have lower incomes than others with a long history of colonial exploitation (for example, Singapore, Malaysia, and Puerto Rico). Among former colonies there is a great variation in present degree of development. Some countries now classified as developing (for example, Egypt, Iran, and China) were at an earlier period of history among the wealthiest and most powerful nations then existing and were colonized after—not before—they lost their dynamism and preeminence. Clearly, factors other than colonialism explain underdevelopment and poverty.

In pointing this out, I am not trying to exonerate the developed countries from partial responsibility for the poverty of the developing countries. But in my view this responsibility arises not so much from the effects of colonialism as from the transfer to the developing countries of programs of public health and hygiene, which sharply reduced their death rates and unleashed a population explosion—forestalling a rise in per capita incomes that would otherwise have occurred. This process began during the colonial period and diluted some of the favorable effects that even colonialism would have had in raising economic levels in the colonies. The reason for this dilution effect is not simply the arithmetic result on per capita GNP of adding one unit of labor and one consumer in a situation characterized by persistent resources away from productivity-enhancing types of investment such as barns and irrigation ditches to consumer-and-welfare-oriented types of investment such as housing, sewers, and hospitals, which primarily serve to enable a larger number of persons to live at an unchanged level of productivity. Accordingly, studies of developing countries have strongly indicated that reductions in population growth might be many times as effective (perhaps 100 times as effective) as traditional development programs in raising per capita incomes.[12] A study I have done myself of 140 developing countries (with under $1000 per capita income) showed a decisive negative correlation between population growth and growth of per capita income.* All this is not conclusive proof, but it does strongly suggest that the way to raise the absolute standard of living of developing countries is to reduce population, which is possible, as we have seen in the previous section of this chapter. By contrast, no simple redistribution of wealth among nations is likely to succeed.

The real chief source of the inequality, difference in productive power, is not an easy thing to redistribute even if there is a willingness to share it, since it resides not only in the prior accumulation of capital but in the acquired skills and work habits of the population, undergirded by an educational and politico-social system that continuously transmits and strengthens those skills and work habits and provides incentives for the continuance of that system.

Likewise, amalgamation of poorer and wealthier nations (if such were possible) might change the gross statistical profile, but the inequalities among the constituent parts of the amalgamated nations would persist. To so raise world GNP to ensure equal prosperity per capita for citizens of developing countries would require an increase from $563 billion (as of 1970) to $7.1 trillion (that is, $7.1 thousand thousand million or 7.1×10^{12}).† This would raise world

---

*See note, p. 12.

† This figure is the product of the estimated developed country per capita GNP of $2,666 and the estimated 1970 developing country popula-

GNP from the actual level in 1970 of $3.2 trillion to a total of $9.7 trillion, that is, by a factor of over three. Thus, if the income gap were suddenly eliminated by the developing countries' achieving developed country income levels, and if population and income levels continued to rise, we would be faced with a world GNP (in 1970 prices) of $9.7 trillion by the end of the century.

With the present composition of GNP, and with 3.5 billion people on earth, a $9.7 trillion GNP* probably implies more than tripling the present rate of natural resource exhaustion, pollution, and general environmental strain. By the year 2000, with normal population and income growth, these figures could be quadrupled.

The adverse environmental effects of the rise in GNP could, of course, be somewhat limited by a qualitative improvement in its composition, involving fewer goods relative to services and goods with a longer serviceable life and absorbing less-scarce materials and energy, concentrating more of the GNP in antipollution measures and devices, taking measures to disperse excessive population concentrations, and finding technological substitutes for scarce raw materials. But the scope for most of these measures, as we have noted, is more limited than sometimes supposed. Thus, it appears unsafe to assume that in practice environmental deterioration will not rise at least as fast as GNP, even if there is considerable improvement in the composition of the GNP.

If, as now seems inevitable, a Survivalist policy requires that some limits on growth be established, or at least on the type of growth pursued, this will no doubt raise quite

---

tion of $2,669 million. [If this bringing of the GNP per capita for developing countries up to the standard of the developed countries had been accomplished in 1976, it would have raised the world GNP by $9.8 trillion (in 1975 dollars), using the same formula—to a total $16.482 trillion, an increase of a factor of 2.5. Editor's note.]

*[Or, it would be a GNP of $16.482 trillion based on the 1976 projection noted in an earlier footnote. Editor's note.]

sharply the question of how the amount of growth in material product that will not endanger the human environment should be shared among the nations. In that case the claims of the developing countries to special consideration will carry great weight. But such claims will be more readily and fruitfully discussed in the context of a general recognition of human interdependence on a small planet and the need for a major change in the human life-style in all countries for the survival of the species. To concentrate now on eliminating or narrowing income gaps of the present kind is to set up an objective that is necessarily doomed to failure and that would create vast and apparently insoluble problems, even if we could somehow come close to achieving it. Moreover, by focusing attention and energy on the wrong goals, it could distract us from the indispensable and urgent tasks that must first be accomplished if progress toward a meaningful and life-sustaining kind of income structure is ever to become possible.

At this point* it may be appropriate to say a few words about the international coordination of dynamic equilibrium policies and, especially, the entry of nontyrannical governments into a community of nations sincerely working for human survival as the top priority objective—and later the adhesion to them of increasingly liberalized governments that were formerly tyrannical. With respect to these problems, survivalists can offer no clear-cut simple solutions— only a few strategic suggestions as to how this goal might best be accomplished.

It must be made clear, however, that nonresistance to tyranny offers no true safeguard for human survival since rival tyrannies with modern weapons can, and if left to their own dynamics would, destroy not only each other but all of humanity. The survival of freedom thus becomes not only a precious value in itself but a probable precondition for the survival of mankind. It is this, alone, that justifies, even

---

*[The author did no more than sketch out the remainder of this section, and what follows is quoted from his summary. Editor's note.]

from a survivalist viewpoint, accepting the risks of nuclear war through the maintenance of effective deterrents, in order to buy time, so that tyrannies may wane and the world be made safe for disarmament—in the sense of the pooling of major armaments under the control of a supranational agency of limited powers (but a monopoly of crucial force) directed by nonpower-seeking persons (discussed in the following chapter), with a supranational status and orientation.

SOCIAL JUSTICE

On a national level Survivalists must also confront the problem analogous to the international question discussed in the previous section, the problem of domestic inequalities. Social justice is a difficult problem but one that is intrinsically soluble, if power-seeking politicians can be prevented from exploiting semantic and ethical confusions in this field to maintain or achieve power. There is a generally ignored, but crucial, difference—and indeed incompatibility— between equality of status and equality of opportunity to achieve unequal statuses. Inequality of status can be limited by government policy, but always at some real cost in incentives and productivity. Humanitarian considerations suggest the desirability of some curb on inequality by setting minimum standards—and in a rich society this might go so far as to achieve the "abolition of poverty" except for large families.

There is a prima facie case for a high degree of equality of opportunity (insofar as achievable without the destruction of other key values), but there is a much weaker case for equalizing status and thereby weakening motivation and productivity, except as needed to achieve two collateral objectives: (1) the establishment of minimum standards for all, so as to avert severe suffering, deprivation, and failure to develop human creative capabilities; and (2) the minimizing of unnecessary consumption of goods in order to conserve resources required by future generations.

As for equality of opportunity and the abolition of classes and castes in society, this is much more readily achievable, though at some costs if pushed too far or too fast. The specific measures required include highly progressive inheritance and gift taxes, which cumulate when the transfer goes beyond a single generation; the discovery and continued subsidization of high levels of ability from early childhood; rigid requirements for equality and objectivity in hiring and promotion at all levels; and a total ban on arbitrary discrimination in any public functions or facilities.

Certain sources of resistance may be anticipated from those threatened by comparative loss of status by those facing competition from those previously not in the race. Most societies will prefer, however, to achieve substantial, but not complete, equality of opportunity in order to protect other significant values.

But what is critical in the pursuit of social justice is the realization that ensuring human survival is now the main issue and must be given an overriding priority over any other objective. The rationale is obvious and compelling: if we survive, we can still pursue social justice; if not, why bother? Everything may turn on whether this question is seriously pondered. For the most damaging opposition to Survivalism is likely to come not from the selfish defenders of the status quo but from the dedicated reformers or revolutionists who feel that directing public attention to goals other than the ones they have already been fighting for would constitute an irrelevancy if not a betrayal. In particular those whose thinking is still influenced by the 125-year-old manifesto of Marx and Engels may be simply incapable of conceiving that anything other than the class struggle (or the ideological or national conflicts proceeding in its name) could be really important or that it might make sense for the classes temporarily to collaborate in saving a world in which, if necessary, the class struggle could later be resumed.

THE OUTLOOK FOR SURVIVALISM

Though the policies advocated in this chapter are un-conventional, they testify to the recognition by Survivalists that our situation is really and truly dangerous and justifies unusual and innovative measures. It is a recognition of that danger and of the urgency of a change in direction that we most need to communicate to the general public.

Public opinion in the United States at least is more receptive than most people suppose. A recent Gallup poll, for example, shows that 81 percent agree and only 10 percent disagree that "our high consumption causes us to pollute the air, the rivers and the seas," while 90 percent agree (and only 5 percent disagree) that "we here in this country will have to find ways to cut back on the amount of things we consume and waste.[13] Such figures reveal a dramatic change of opinion in just a few years. And when ratios get to be over 80 percent, the experts consider them to be too strong to reflect merely short-term temporary fluctu-ations.

But how can such opinion shifts be translated into action? I count on two major forces. The first is the contin-ued agitation of Survivalists. The second is the progressive worsening of the crisis. With some ups and downs, I believe, inflation *and* unemployment (the supposed incompatibles) will remain very serious. Energy shortages will continually threaten to stop industrial (and much agricultural) activity. Famines and epidemics of pollution will become common-place. Terrorism, already commonplace, will become ever more threatening as the terrorists obtain more and more deadly weapons. And we shall have wars—or confrontations threatening war—over remaining stocks of high-quality, low-cost resources. Therefore, the public, which already accepts the need for change, will become more receptive to making those changes that can end the crisis.

Already there are grounds for hope. The ecologists, the pacifists, and the social reformers of all stripes, despite their obvious weaknesses, have been able to exert considerable influence. Much, therefore, may be expected of a broad movement, unified by world events, based on a solid scientific foundation, and inspired by the most elemental sort of idealism: loyalty to one's own species and concern for the fate of one's own descendants. Such a movement could look to institutions such as the United Nations and the Club of Rome for support. Within a short time Survivalists may well enlist the sympathies of a majority of the world's scientists and scholars and a good number of its religious, business, and political leaders—making it the major social movement for the remainder of the century. By the beginning of the next century, the climate of opinion might be ready for the fundamental changes in laws, and social institutions required to cope effectively with the crises that await us. If so, the coming age will appear in retrospect as having achieved the most fundamental revolution in history—the one that gave the human race a second chance.

EXCURSUS ON "THE INFLATION-UNEMPLOYMENT TRADE-OFF"[14]

It used to be said that a parrot could learn economics if you could just teach him to say "supply" and "demand." Today it might with equal justice be claimed that you could teach a parrot the principles of modern economic policy if you could just get him to repeat endlessly the term *Phillips curve*. The Phillips curve shows a statistically negative relationship between the rate of unemployment and the rate of inflation: when the unemployment rate is high, the rate of inflation tends to be low, and vice versa. Upon this rock have modern policy makers built their church. Disagreements are mainly over at what point the trade-off should be made.

Some, who are more concerned with the vast waste and human misery of heavy unemployment—and its political risks—are willing to accept more inflation. Others, who are more concerned about the dangers of further stoking the fires of inflation, are willing to put up with 7 percent unemployment, or more, for years, if necessary, if this will help moderate inflation. But none of them doubt that this dismal trade-off is inescapable. One is reminded of the original "dismal science" economics of Ricardo and Malthus, with its wages fund doctrine that "proved" that the wages of common labor could never rise above a bare subsistence level—so that any attempt to improve the conditions of the masses was hopeless.

I would like to challenge this commonly held view. To be sure, the Phillips curve does have some statistical basis and charts a genuine (though by no means close) relationship of varying intensity that has been observed in certain countries in a certain historical period. Nevertheless, the statistical basis is somewhat weak to carry such an immense policy load. We have no way of determining within what range of variation it will remain true, nor for how long. Furthermore, it simply charts a relationship; it does not really explain it. And some of the institutional forces that may have been responsible for temporarily creating that relationship may now be breaking down. For example, as strikebreaking becomes institutionally less and less feasible and as trade unions become more and more strongly organized with more and more political power, they become less and less deterred from striking to achieve wage increases, even in periods of heavy unemployment.

My initial observation is that ever since 1950 the U.S. cost of living has risen every single year,* even in periods of recession and when raw material costs have declined. Thus, recession and unemployment can no longer stop inflation but, at most, only slow it down. A second observation is that recently new forces appear to be at work to give an explosive quality to inflation: inflation has appeared at unparalleled rates *despite* unemployment rates exceeding anything seen since the Great Depression.

---

*Revised estimates do show a 0.4 percent decline in consumer prices in 1955, but the more comprehensive price index of the Implicit Deflator for the GNP shows a 1.3 percent increase.

Obviously, the Phillips curve tells only a part of the complex truth about the relationship between unemployment and inflation. To achieve true prosperity, we will have to give equal recognition to the rest of the story, which has so far been largely ignored. The simplistic Phillips curve approach makes it appear that the only possible way to stop inflation is to create a lot of slack in the economy by means of tight money and cuts in government spending. Thus, interest rates have been raised sharply, and the money supply, corrected for price increases, was cut by a tenth. And—though this is not generally realized—real federal expenditures on goods and services (that is, outlays corrected for price increases) have been cut by 28 percent between 1968 and 1974.* Now for the first time since World War II, even the expenditures of state and local governments are beginning to decline in real terms. This did succeed in creating a slack, all right: production was off by a tenth, and the unemployment rate rose by a seventh. Yet prices kept rising. The existence of major recession and violent inflation at the same time points to a basic weakness in the whole theory.

These deflationary policies seek to cut the total of spending with the classical notion that if inflation is too many dollars chasing too few goods, then if you reduce the number of dollars chasing the goods, you are bound to moderate the inflation. What is not recognized is that if goods are produced only in order to be sold, then if you cut back the size of the markets, you are likely at the same time to cut back the amount of goods produced and offered for sale—in which case the gap between the amount of goods available and the number of dollars chasing them may be little if at all narrowed, and inflation may by no means have been ended. By this route it may take a very long time indeed to eliminate the excess of dollars over goods, and it is an

---

*[The figure between 1968 and 1978 has remained in the vicinity of 28 percent. Editor's note.]

extremely painful and dangerous way to do it, in terms of lost production and lives wasted and embittered by unnecessary unemployment.

What I should like now to suggest is the novel theory that a more effective way to end inflation (and to produce full economic recovery at the same time) is to produce not less but *more*—sufficiently more so that supply overtakes demand and begins to drive prices down—while making sure by way of controls and taxation that after-tax income and demand do not rise too quickly, especially for items not essential for the national welfare.

How could this be done? Hitherto we have thought solely in terms of achieving the right level of aggregate demand, and we assumed that this by itself would ensure the achievement of full employment. If for Phillips curve reasons we felt we had to sacrifice full employment, we believed that it would at least give us a tolerable level of unemployment plus price stability. What we now begin to realize is that even if we could agree on the "right" level of aggregate demand and could arrange our policies so that it was attained and maintained, this would still meet only half the problem. The other half is the question of the elasticity of supply—how supply reacts to changes in aggregate demand. This is something we can no longer assume will take care of itself.

In fact in highly concentrated industries (where the bulk of the product is produced by a small number of producers), there is a persistent tendency to respond to demand increases by raising prices instead of increasing output at the previous prices. And when demand slumps, production costs rise because of suboptimal use of fixed-cost production facilities and institutional difficulties in making any comparable offsetting savings on wages.

With higher costs producers feel they must quote higher prices to conserve their margins and enable them to finance increasingly expensive plant replacements. They can usually get the higher prices, or at least maintain high prices, despite stagnant or shrinking demand, by the use of their market power: the relatively few producers responsible for a large share of the market recognize that price cuts leading to retaliatory price wars would ultimately benefit none of the contenders and might paradoxically even get them into trouble with the Antitrust Division of the Justice Department as evidence of destructive competition with an intent to monopolize. Therefore, they tacitly agree to keep prices stable or even to increase them to reflect higher costs—plus a little extra.

Thus, in good times and bad there is a continued tendency for prices to rise. Moreover, the strongly organized trade unions that are particularly powerful in the concentrated industries are regularly given wage increases far in excess of their increases in productivity, resulting in further cost increases that are passed on to the public in the form of higher prices.

There are two main arguments against this whole point of view. First, it is said that once the interested parties have achieved their optimum oligopoly price, they have no incentive for further price increases. Hence, this factor would not explain continuously rising prices. This argument ignores the gradualness with which market power is acquired and strengthened and the tentative and slow way in which it is learned how to use it effectively and to circumvent the obstacles established by antitrust. It is not even clear that the optimum oligopoly price is determinate. If it is, it is certainly not easy to recognize. It is not surprising that it should be approached via the respectable technique of successive approximations. Also, it keeps being pushed up by rising labor costs.

The second argument is that statistical studies show no positive correlation between the degree of concentration and the extent of price increases. Indeed, industries where four companies control more than half the industry show lower price increases than industries where four companies control less than half of the industry's output.[15] This is a serious argument, but it does not rigorously demonstrate that market power may not be a factor in inflation. For the large companies in highly concentrated industries may make sufficient productivity gains so that they could provide moderate wage increases and maintain profits even with price cuts. If instead they provide high wage increases and medium price increases, they set an influential example for other less productive companies. The smaller companies in less concentrated industries may have quite sufficient market power to exact sizable price increases; in their cases they must, first of all, pay the higher prices for their industrial inputs to be bought from the concentrated industries; second, they must pay more or less the same wage increases as already announced in the concentrated industries, even though productivity gains may be minimal. In that case prices may have to be raised even more than in the concentrated industries to achieve any profits at all. Thus, the fact that their prices may rise slightly more than in the highly concentrated industries does not really prove that market power is not an important transmission belt for inflation.

A true prosperity policy would therefore attempt more than to achieve the right level of demand. It would pay equal attention to ensure that supply was freely and adequately responsive to demand. Obviously, this is no easy task. The general principle involved is that no wage increases should be permitted in unionized industries in excess of productivity increases and that no price increases should be permitted in concentrated industries in excess of demonstrable increases in costs. (Perhaps such excessive increases might not be barred in advance but retroactively nullified by a 100 percent tax on such excessive wage increases and on profits derived from such price increases.) Trade unions could still win real wage increases, but only by helping to bring about productivity increases that made it possible to produce more with the same number of workers. Companies could still increase their after-tax profits, but only by increasing their production and sales or cutting costs—not by raising prices.

Obviously, it is a lot easier to propound such a general policy than it would be to specify its detailed mode of operation and enforcement. And if (as is likely) this would require more regulatory agencies, there are obvious dangers that they might be "captured" by the industries they were intended to regulate, as have so many other regulatory commissions. The difficulties are obvious. Clearly, substantial governmental reforms would be required to curtail corruption and influence peddling and to ensure that the additional governmental powers would be properly used. But if this is what it takes to eliminate inflationary recession (as I believe to be the case), then it is worth it. Our government takes incredible pains over such matters as social security, labor organizations, restraints on agricultural production, security regulation, et cetera, all of which are worth doing but none of which are remotely as important as the elimination of inflationary recessions.

We must, once and for all, abandon laissez-faire and recognize that government, though ill-equipped to run particular industries, is essential for mobilizing a national consensus on priorities and for establishing a network of incentives that will ensure its implementation. It now begins to appear that this is almost as important in solving our short-term as our long-term problems.

NOTES

1. Stephen Enke, "Economic Aspects of Slowing Population Growth," *Economic Journal* 76 (March 1966): 44–56; idem, *Description of the Economic Demographic Model* (Santa Barbara, Calif.: TEMPO, 1971).

2. See Timothy King, "The Measurement of the Economic Benefits from Family Planning Projects and Programs," Working Paper no. 71 (Washington, D.C.: World Bank, Department of Economics, March 23, 1970), p. 6n.

3. Successful research results on animals were reported by R. Yanagimachi, J. Winkelhake, and G. L. Nicolson in the *Proceedings of the National Academy of Sciences* 73 (July 1976): 2405–08.

4. John H. G. Pierson, *Essays on Full Employment 1942-1972* (Metuchen, N. J.: Scarecrow Press, 1973).

5. See, for example, Emile Benoit, "Net Investment, Con-

sumption and Full Employment," *American Economic Review* 34 (December 1944): 871 and 878; idem, "Full Employment: Its Economic and Legal Aspects," *Antioch Review* 5 (Fall 1945); and my debate with Senator Paul Douglas, idem, "A Tax Cut Now?" *New Republic* 147, no. 6-7 (August 13, 1962): 15.

6. See, for example, James Cicarelli, "Whatever Happened to the Turbine Car?" *Bulletin of Atomic Scientists* 30 (December 1974): 24-29.

7. Ford Foundation, Energy Policy Project, *A Time to Choose: America's Energy Future. Final Report by the Energy Policy Project of the Ford Foundation* (Boston, Mass.: Ballinger, 1974).

8. Garrett Hardin, "The Tragedy of the Commons," *Science* 162 (December 1968): 1243-48.

9. Arthur McCormach, "Population and Development at Bucharest and After," *International Development Review* 17 (1975): 14–19.

10. U.S. Arms Control and Disarmament Agency, *World Military Expenditures and Arms Transfers: 1967-1976* (Washington, D.C. U.S. Government Printing Office, 1978), p. 20.

11. A discussion of the limitations of such estimates may be found in Emile Benoit, *Disarmament and World Economic Interdependence* (New York: Columbia University Press, 1966), chap. 2. The developing countries are identified by the U.S. Arms Control and Disarmament Agency (ACDA) as including all of Africa except South Africa, all of Asia except Japan, and all of the Middle East and Latin America, whereas the developed countries include the United States, Canada, Japan, South Africa, Australia, and New Zealand and all of Europe except Greece, Turkey, Bulgaria, Albania, Spain, and Yugoslavia, which are viewed as developing.

12. Enke, "Economic Effects of Slowing Population Growth," pp. 44-56; and idem, *Description of the Economic Demographic Model.*

13. Quoted in *New Yorker* 51 (December 15, 1975): 33.

14. Excerpted from Emile Benoit, "The Inflation-Unemployment Tradeoff and Full Economic Recovery," *American Journal of Economics and Sociology* 34 (October 1975): 337-44 (which was adapted from a public lecture on "The Political Economy of Shortages" given at the University of California, Santa Barbara, on April 28, 1975).

15. See Steven Lastgarten, *Industrial Concentration and Inflation* (Washington, D.C.: American Institute for Public Policy Research, 1975).

5

Objections and resistances

D ynamic equilibrium and the rest of the Survivalist
program will never be implemented without a
struggle. In this chapter I shall discuss some of the
difficulties Survivalists must expect to encounter.

FEAR OF TOTALITARIANISM

There is likely to arise the fear that dynamic equilibrium
would involve a great expansion in the power and size of
government—possibly socialism or even dictatorship. None
of this is remotely justified, in my opinion. But the objection
is likely to carry much weight, and so perhaps a word of
explanation is in order.

We must remember that the additional government
activities required under dynamic equilibrium are intended
neither to equalize incomes nor to eliminate the "wastes of

competition" by government operation of industry. They are needed solely because various negative externalities (which, as I have explained, are by definition not self-eliminating in the free market) turn out to be far more important than previously realized and, in fact, threaten human survival. Government must intervene to the extent necessary to motivate people not to take the actions producing such negative externalities.

Such interventions may, and should, be democratically approved, adopted, and controlled like any other government program. Moreover, government does not need to use any powers other than those that are already in use, such as taxation, subsidization, government contracts, or licensing and regulation of industries that are insufficiently competitive or that are in the public interest.

Those who basically distrust government on principle may not approve of such a world. But they should seriously ask themselves whether there is any realistic chance of avoiding a great increase in government intervention in the future, with mounting pressures of pollution, overpopulation, and inflationary shortages of good and basic materials and with rising crime and terrorism and recurrent fears of war. If government intervention is unplanned and not part of an open and deliberately adopted public policy, it is likely to become increasingly secretive, arbitrary, and corrupt—with desperate efforts by the rich and powerful to protect themselves from difficult adjustments and sacrifices and to shift such adjustments and sacrifices to others with less influence. Such a course will inevitably undermine public confidence in governments and institutions and generate rising tensions. Indeed, we already seem to have moved a considerable distance along this path.

Nor would dynamic equilibrium require the abolition or drastic modification of capitalism. Modern capitalism I view as very different from mere laissez-faire. It involves private ownership and management of most productive enterprises, under the guidance of the profit motive, but it does not assume that this will automatically, as by a guiding hand, promote the public interest, unless there is strong government intervention to ensure that businesses cannot make profits except by providing genuine services compatible with long-term social goals.

Naturally, a capitalist society with a strong Survivalist orientation would be quite different from what we have now. Government would have a much more fundamental and activist role, serving not only as an agent for expressing, reconciling, and balancing particular interests but acting on behalf of the common interest, and particularly on behalf of future generations. In any event the more activist government need not necessarily be larger, because, as previously suggested, implementation of a full-employment program, which is part of the Survivalist agenda, would end the necessity for much of the antipoverty bureaucracy, so that as the new government bureaucracies grew, they would only replace other shrinking bureaucracies, leaving little net difference in size.

Moreover, the free market has always required the supervision of a sizable and active government apparatus. Only government intervention to enforce competition, and to regulate natural monopolies and highly concentrated industries with administered prices, could ensure the realization of the theoretical benefits of a free market. And it has become increasingly obvious that government subventions (explicit or via tax allowances) for building pyramids, churches, palaces, public housing, and transportation and energy systems have historically been a major force for growth—and that such acts involve government initiatives rather than responses to the free market.

While capitalists (and others) might prefer a continuance of unrestricted growth, once it is determined that this would be incompatible with the interests (indeed the survival) of the society in the long run, capitalism could function quite well under a set of guidelines intended to promote dynamic equilibrium. Capitalism functioned quite successfully in wartime when there was little growth in the private sector and the product mix was subject to rapid change. It is

communism, rather than capitalism, that has chiefly emphasized rapid growth in recent years. Indeed, dynamic equilibrium with its sharply rising environmental costs (taxes on
raw materials and pollution) and rapidly changing product
mix would make high-caliber management more essential
than ever—and it is only capitalism that historically can
provide this.

But would not restraints on luxury goods destroy
capitalist incentives? One cannot answer with complete
assurance, but I doubt it. Max Weber has taught us that
capitalism originated not in the desire to consume wealth
but in the desire to accumulate it and to demonstrate
effective stewardship by managing it profitably. So long as
large profits and large salaries are allowed to the successful
and may be used to exercise power through investment and
management (as well as to purchase extra services and to
win prestige as status indicators), then they may continue to
motivate individuals adequately, even though their capacity
to buy luxurious consumer goods and housing may be
drastically reduced. (As I have indicated, a shift to different
sorts of employment in fields having to do with new forms
of transportation, methanol refining, R&D, et cetera would
offset the unemployment resulting from any sharp cut in
production of luxury items presently used as status indicators.)

It would be the responsibility of Survivalists to allay
such legitimate doubts; we do not seek to change either the
country's mode of government or its economy.

OPPOSITION GROUPS

There are groups that Survivalists will just have to
resign themselves to fighting. These include: (1) the obvious
vested interests; (2) those religious, ideological, and academic groups that either proclaim that nothing basic is, or
could be, wrong or that they control the only effective cure;
(3) certain jealous reformist and revolutionary groups that

are fearful of competition in their struggle for public attention and for reformist financial support; and (4) governments that, while proclaiming their exclusive responsibility
for the long-term welfare of the people they represent, are
in fact too concerned with winning and keeping office—and
winning victories over national or ideological rivals—to care
about anything else.

PSYCHOLOGICAL ELEMENTS IN THE SURVIVAL CRISIS

Beyond the inertia of institutions that resist change,
beyond the rational doubts that must be dealt with by
argument, and beyond the predictable opposition of the
groups just mentioned, Survivalists will find themselves
constantly encountering very elusive but deep-seated resistances, which can only be laid to human nature. These
resistances do not intimate that human nature is ineradica-
bly stubborn or perverse; quite the contrary: they are what
has made the human race a success up to this point in
history. Let us consider them.

Modern ethology and sociobiology teach us that behavioral patterns can be as deeply rooted in genetic factors as
morphological features. That is to say, such basic behavioral
patterns as eating, resting, communicating, mating, and
fighting are supported by inherited predispositions; and
although in some degree they are mediated and modified by
the cultural environment, they do, nevertheless, have a
tendency under favorable environmental conditions to develop along certain characteristic lines for each species
within a normal range of variations. They resist modification beyond this range, and patterns of behavior falling
within this range are as much limited by genetic endow-
ments, and as characteristic of a given species or subspecies,
as are the shape, size, color, and chemical composition of
their various organs.

Mankind, while showing a much higher degree of

cultural modifiability of such hereditary behavioral patterns than other animals, is nevertheless also subject to some limitations on normal variability. To be sure, behavioral variations even beyond these limits do occasionally occur, just as clearly abnormal variations also occur on the morphological level, such as children being born with six fingers or no legs. But such mutations, if dysfunctional, tend not to be reproduced and thus tend to remain exceptional. Therefore, even if a few saintly or merely eccentric humans have voluntarily practiced total asceticism, or total silence, or total self-abasement, this was accomplished only at considerable sacrifice of typically human qualities. And if such behavior were widely enough imitated, the race would expire.

In fact it has not expired. On the contrary, the human race has become such an enormous success that it now threatens the viability of its own environment. That success was dependent on the range of behavioral patterns that made its success possible.

The earliest pattern, it seems, was hunting. By far the largest part of man's existence, qua man, has been spent as a hunter. Man's survival has therefore depended primarily on his ability to overpower and eat other animals (including sometimes other men) in order to stay alive. In that setting, a lust to dominate and subdue had strong survival value, while scruples over the taking of life, or empathy with the object dominated, would have been highly dysfunctional. The greed for power, being crucial to survival, was reinforced in the human genetic structure by the processes of natural and sexual selection. Such evidence as we have of contemporary primitive people living in a preagricultural culture seems to support this thesis. In such hunting societies, scruples over the taking of life (except of fellow tribesmen) seem notably absent, and the successful hunter is accorded the highest material rewards and the best choice of women—being thus most likely to survive and to have numerous offspring.

The invention of agriculture made it possible for many more people to live in a given area, and the investment in clearing, tillage, fertilization, and sowing the seed required continued residence in that area to reap the benefits of this investment. This led to the emergence of property rights in land as well as in things, animals, and people. In time there emerged a warrior-landowner-governing class laying claim to large areas by right of conquest—sanctioned by God's supposed choice of the victor in "trial by combat." The cultivators and herdsman had to provide these lords with a portion of the fruits of their labor, either in the form of unpaid labor by slaves, customary tithes and tributes by serfs, or rents and taxes by free men. The exactions were regarded as justified both by absolute rights of ownership and as appropriate compensation for the risks and hardships of the warriors in protecting the underlying classes against invaders and despoilers.

Thus, the agricultural economy brought about a diversification and specialization of behavioral patterns. Generally speaking, it was the most ferocious warriors and ruthlessly exploitative slaveowners and landlords, as well as the most ambitious, cunning, and unscrupulous politico-military overlords, that tended to gain control over larger and larger areas, to exact larger and larger surpluses of food and other goods for themselves and their families, and to produce the largest number of surviving (legitimate and illegitimate) offspring. On the other hand, in the subject classes there may have been some attenuation of the power drive, as the more self-assertive types that offered resistance to being exploited were increasingly driven into outlawry and vagabondage or had their life-span shortened in other ways. On balance agriculture probably did not much affect the average strength of the human greed for power, but it did tend to concentrate more of it in the dominant classes, which determined what happened.

As for the industrial era, it has simply been too short to have had any significant effect on man's hereditary power drive. We are talking, after all, of fewer than a dozen generations—even in the areas where industrialization first began. For whatever environmental or genetic reasons the individual roles are assigned, the general allocation of social function and personality holds to this day. In virtually all societies, we see successors of the cultivators and herdsmen and of the warrior-landowners. The life of those in the first group is still predominantly a matter of avoiding danger, gathering food, feeding, breeding, and socializing. Whether they are actually hunters, herdsmen, peasants, or factory or office workers, they spend most of their energies on meeting the same fundamental biological needs as other animals. Essentially followers rather than leaders or initiators, they live ordinarily in accordance with the customs and fashions of their times, by doing as others do and as others expect them to do.

The successors of the warrior-landowners tend to be more intelligent, but that is not the fundamental difference. The main difference, rather, is that they have more strongly developed their acquisitiveness, their combativeness, their appetite for dominance, their ambition, and their farsightedness. Along with these go a greatly increased individualism, daring, and hardihood and a willingness to initiate, to do the unexpected, to be different from others, to encounter and accept hostility, and to take risks for the sake of the prizes to be won. Basically, they have specialized in controlling the activities of other men by various forms of psychological manipulation, such as force, threat, promises, setting an admired example, fraud, rhetoric, or negotiation and bargaining. As different as these various modes of influencing behavior may appear (and as important as these differences may be from an ethical viewpoint), they do have some important underlying psychological similarities: they all involve winning control or ascendency over the actions of others for the achievement of material advantages and also, usually, to a greater or lesser extent, for the pleasure of "winning," getting the better of the bargain, achieving or exercising power, being "top dog," being accorded deference, or simply experiencing the pleasure of running things.

This division of psychological and behavioral patterns between ruling and subject classes, though doubtless responsible for endless suffering and misery, has served the survival of the race reasonably well. From having been at first a miserable insecure handful, our race has become far and away the most successful of the terrestrial vertebrates—whether measured by area of habitation, ability to control and dominate other species, or average life expectancy relative to maximum genetically achievable longevity, or possibly even if measured in sheer tonnage.

All, this, however, relates solely to the past. Traits that contribute to the survival of a species under a given set of conditions may hasten its demise when these conditions change. Thus, the vast bulk of the dinosaurs made them formidable predators and the dominant species for millions of years; but with climatic and other changes they disappeared relatively quickly. And there is a long list of other extinct species, each of which was a success story for a while. There are now abundant indications that *Homo sapiens* may soon join this list unless human development can successfully adapt to the new circumstances we confront.

These new circumstances, outlined in Chapters 2 and 3, present appalling threats if the world continues to be guided, as it presently is, by those with abnormal power drives. The pressures to do violence to fellow men, to the environment, and to future generations are too fierce, and the technology with which to do that violence is altogether too potent and inviting. In an era when only cooperation can avert conflict over scarce resources, the power greedy are all too likely to fight over them. Since virtually all governments, as presently constituted, are the creations of the power-greedy classes, the real functions and interests of those governments, as stated, are the retention of power, the triumph of nation and ideology over rivals, and the compromising and adjusting of conflicting internal interests. They lack the time, energy, and concern to make more than perfunctory gestures toward advancing the true long-term welfare of the human groups they represent. In other words evolution has seen to it that rulers are not Survivalists. Thus, it has become necessary to dispossess the rulers.

Any such project, of course, swarms with difficulties, the most crushing, from a practical point of view, being the basic problem of taking even a part of their power from those who are by their nature the most interested and skillful in obtaining and retaining power. Who, after all, will bell the cat? Evolution has rendered the successors of the cultivators and herdsmen generally unfit for the task.

Fortunately, there is another social or behavioral group, neither serf nor overlord, made up in primitive societies of highly skilled artisan-inventors, medicine men, wise old advisers, and authorities on rituals, customs, myths, and kinship structures—and, in our world, of practitioners of the arts and the learned professions. Historically and presently, the power greedy have dominated the intellectual class, gaining control over and exploiting those innovations of the intellectuals that have practical utility. Today this ceases to be merely an inconvenience for the intellectuals; it is, rather, a grave source of danger for mankind as well.

It is from this class, therefore, that Survivalists are most likely to arise, at least initially, and from this class that new leaders would have to come. And I believe they can. It is a persistent myth of our time that only "politicians" can run governments. To be sure, this is true enough of the present *kind* of government. Only power-greedy politicians are sufficiently in tune with this game to operate handily in such an environment. But if, as I have argued, we now need a very different sort of government, one that regards helping humanity turn the corner and avoid its threatened self-destruction as its primary mission, then we will need, correspondingly, a very different set of persons to run such a government—persons with a passion for intellectual integrity, with an abiding curiosity for how things work, and with a fundamental commitment to helping mankind survive. It is only they, not the politicians, who could make this sort of government work.

Knowing who will bell the cat, we still face the question of how to bell the cat. Ideally, but impractically, politicians, lawyers, businessmen, military men, and trade union leaders could simply be excluded from the top jobs, and only physicians, scientists, architects, engineers, educators, artists, craftsmen, ministers, et cetera could hold office. More realistically, the prospect would be for Survivalists to seek to gain direct or indirect control of events, despite their competitive disadvantages and their preference for other activities to the wielding of power. The crisis is too grave to be left to the politicians.

Another legacy of our evolution that Survivalists will need to recognize is the individual and social fear of death, a more fundamental force than is generally recognized. Like other animals, man has a genetic predisposition to avoid death, accompanied by perturbations inwardly experienced as fear. (I would be glad to substitute more circuitous language for the sake of behaviorists, but we all know what I mean.) Such fear has played a role, too obvious to bother setting forth, in the evolutionary process.

However, because man has been able to recognize the ubiquity and inevitability of death, and is endowed with exceptional capacity for memory and foresight, he might find this fear immobilizing if he had not developed certain mechanisms for dealing with it. The most common of such mechanisms is repression. Elaborate defense mechanisms have been developed to repress awareness of the fear of death, for instance, through religious doctrines and institutions that portray death as merely the gateway to eternal life; men half-persuaded that death is merely an illusion find it easier not to think about it until it is imminent.

Our belief in the exponential growth of our societies and of our race seems to be a collective manifestation of the same fear. I have discussed what I call the exponential growth syndrome earlier, in Chapters 2 and 3. It is the modification of attitudes, ideologies, standards, and ways of life on the assumption that exponential growth is the normal condition and must continue indefinitely, since everyone's welfare depends on it. The obvious fact that, in a world of limited dimensions and resources, exponential growth *cannot* go on indefinitely—or even for very long—is something that, like our awareness of death, is repressed. As with death we rely on magical solutions or outright unreasonable denial to make the inevitable disappear or seem illusory. Thus, as if by some grim jest, those who write about the danger of human destruction are more likely to bore than to horrify their readers. There has been so much written, some of it extremely inaccurate, about the dangers to human survival that the "cry wolf" syndrome has now completely taken over. I rather doubt that a signed statement of all the world's Nobel prize winners to the effect that there was a 99 percent probability that mankind would be completely destroyed within ten years would attract any great public attention.

Thus, attempts to confront the realities and to discover how they might be transcended are nit-picked and ridiculed or otherwise discredited. The Club of Rome's 1972 study, *The Limits to Growth* (conducted by the Meadows team),[1] applied the powerful methods of computer-aided systems analysis to basic questions of ecology, resources, and population and concluded that exponential growth could not be sustained much longer—that humanity would either deliberately level off its growth rate or overshoot the objective carrying capacity of the environment and collapse to a far smaller population and industrial base. What was most startling about the report was the assertion—backed up by elaborate estimates—that this outcome was something that would happen not in the distant future but probably within the next 70 years, that is, within the lifetime of children born to its readers. One of the enormous advantages of systems analysis is that it enables one to test how sensitive one's conclusions are to particular assumptions and conditions by progressively relaxing them. The study made use of this advantage by assuming progressively: that we could by deep ocean mining, use of nuclear energy, et cetera multiply several fold the available reserves of most raw materials; that we could, by recycling, use only one-fourth as much of them per unit of industrial output as we do today; that we could reduce pollution per unit of output to one-fourth of present levels; that we could perfect birth control 100 percent, so that no unwanted children were born; that we could, through the Green Revolution, double the average yield on all cultivated acreage; et cetera. It turned out that not even the simultaneous application of all these highly optimistic assumptions changed the essentials of the foregoing picture or would delay the threatened collapse by more than a few decades. The report concluded: "The basic behavior mode of the world system is exponential growth of population and capital followed by collapse."

Academic orthodoxy rushed to criticize the report. Norman MacRae[2] came forth with a brilliant critique, for instance, that nonetheless boiled down at bottom to a blind faith that technology can move mountains, with reminders that the growth potentials of the past would not have been predictable on the basis of what was then known. But such retrospective analogical arguments can do no more than remind us that it is always possible to make mistakes. They do not really prove that the mistakes are necessarily biased in the direction of underestimating the possibilities of finding technological solutions to our problems. Others made much of the fact that the report's projection of ecological disaster within 125 years would be falsified if one changed some of the assumptions. Yet the usual conclusion of the critics. that therefore the dangers were illusory revealed their own underlying biases. For if they had taken their own assumptions and traced out how much difference they would make—as in several cases I have done—they would have found that their more favorable assumptions would simply delay the pending catastrophe for a period that was essentially trivial in relation to man's prior existence and future aspirations.

Similarly illuminating were three responses to a recent

paper of mine on dynamic equilibrium. The editor of a leading economic journal wrote me an enthusiastic concurrence but considered that the perils we face were even greater and the necessary measures to cope with them even harsher than I had suggested. A distinguished congressman deeply involved in conservation and environmental affairs stated that my paper "ought to receive some attention and favorable action." But the editor of a widely read intellectual journal refused to publish the piece because he was not "persuaded by the conventional wisdom of the day concerning the shortage of natural resources. My guess is that the crisis is widely exaggerated for a variety of tendentious political reasons."

The comment of this editor seems to me to point to the deeper source of the difficulty. The heart of his resistance to what I had to say—his suspicion that the crisis was "widely exaggerated for a variety of tendentious political reasons," his obvious preference of comforting illusion to sober reality—is related to the repressive mode of reaction to the fear of death. Bolstered by the orthodox religious doctrine that an all-powerful and loving God has promised man eternal life and told him to "go forth, multiply, and dominate the earth," the true believer cannot entertain the thought that his ultimate heirs might receive only a wasteland. Thus, a climate of opinion is developed in which it is unthinkable that built-in shortages really exist, since this would uncover the illusions by means of which we repress our fear of death.

For Survivalism to succeed, Survivalists must therefore prepare to transcend, and to aid others to transcend, the fear of racial extinction, which paradoxically threatens to produce it.

CONCLUSION

Having analyzed the likely resistances, we will need to formulate a strategy as to how they may best be dissipated, undermined, circumvented, deflected, resisted, or—if necessary—ignored without too much loss of momentum.

Those actually involved in the fray will be better able than I to choose their specific tactics for doing so.

No one can say, at this point, what chance Survivalism has of succeeding. All we can say is that man's evolutionary effort to adjust and survive will be wholly bound up in this effort. It seems improper in any case to speculate on such a matter. When the house is on fire, it is not for us to speculate on the odds for getting out but to mobilize every effort and every resource to get out and to minimize the damage. The human race has faced and mastered crises of survival before—primarily through the use of its two great survival tools: intelligence and flexibility. These are just what are needed now.

When one looks at history and reflects on the incredible sacrifices and valor displayed on occasion to eliminate relatively small injustices or to advance by a few years reforms that would soon have come anyway, it is hard to imagine that courage and determination will be lacking to fight for the major changes required for human survival. The chief difficulty is the novelty of the form that the danger takes, which makes it harder to mobilize the self-protective instincts, since the nature of the threat is not immediately apparent. If, however, the Survivalist movement can clarify and dramatize this threat, then mankind's deep will to live will mobilize the efforts required to carry through the necessary reforms. And those who participate in this movement will know that the vital evolutionary destiny of their race is working itself out through their efforts and sacrifices—which is the deepest satisfaction of which man is capable.

In the already classic words of Fred Ikle: "There is time—but not much time."

NOTES

1. D. H. Meadows, D. L. Meadows, J. Randers, W. W. Behrens III, *The Limits to Growth* (New York: Universe Books, 1972).

2. Norman MacRae, *Economist* 243 (January 22, 1972): 67.

POSTSCRIPT

T he individual must in any case die, but the question is seriously asked whether he can in some degree rob death of its sting by contributing to the perpetuation of the kind of life he represents. In other animal species, this may require the sacrifice of life in battle or in diverting marauders, and during the larger part of man's existence, this was largely true also of our own species. In the twentieth century, however, it has become clear that the genetic makeup of most surviving groups is much alike and that the destructive power of modern weapons is so great as to imperil the survival of all groups in the event of a major war. What is quintessentially important, then, is the survival of human culture; and the new technology of communication and recording may even make it possible for more and more of the cultural contributions of individuals to enter into the historical record and to be handed down to future generations.

If I can help to make a better world for my children and their children to live in, and leave some enduring record of

---

[On November 9, 1977, less than six months before his death, the author delivered these remarks to the University Seminar on Death at Columbia University. Editor's note.]

how I tried to help, this is all the immortality to which I aspire, and I shall be content, when the time comes, and when so many of my experiences are painful ones, to cease having new experiences. Even unending joy would ultimately become a bit of a bore. Once I have reached life's summit and have enjoyed all I am capable of enjoying, and if I can have the satisfaction of having helped make human life more secure, then I shall be glad to stop. I may still fear death, but I shall recognize it as an instinctive reaction—a heritage of my animal nature, which my human reason assures me I need not take too seriously. Indeed, to die with dignity and a sense of transcending one's instinctive fears is one of the supreme triumphs of *human* life.

EDITOR'S NOTE

When the author, my father, died suddenly on May 4, 1978, he left behind, unfinished, the book that he had hoped would be the crowning effort of his retirement. All of us who gathered together to console each other for our loss agreed that if his work could be salvaged, it should, not only because it had been transcendently important to my father but also because we believed in the importance of the book itself. I was chosen to do the salvaging.

I found a large miscellaneous collection of materials, some in successive drafts, many overlapping, some published or delivered in talks, and many simply in rough typescript or holograph. There were also two rough outlines of the book, both clearly out of date, useful to demonstrate more the scope of the projected book than its actual arrangement as my father seems to have conceived it toward the end. Of some of the materials called for by the outline, I could find no trace, and it is my conviction that my father never tried to write those parts. But for most sections of the outline, there was too much material rather than too little.

I found myself on the horns of a dilemma. On the one hand, I wanted to produce a concise, well-organized text, such as my father had often explicitly stated he expected this book to be; on the other hand, I wanted to be true to a mass of material that, before editing, was neither well organized nor concise.

In the end, and somewhat inevitably, I fell back upon the technique of picking one text that I felt to be the latest or best for each passage and collating that basic text with other versions of that passage to determine if there was something of value in those other versions that ought to be inserted into, or substituted for, the phrasing of the basic text. This frequently seemed to be the case, and I made such alterations freely.

I made numerous other changes as well, smoothing out the style, reorganizing parts of essays to make the book progress logically, cutting out redundancies, and writing in bridges to connect one line of thought with another. I had to do these things; I was assembling a book. My father, had he lived, would have no doubt taken the same liberties with his own writings. In any case, I can assure the reader that there is nothing here my father would not have recognized as his own. This is his book, not mine.

That is not to say that this is altogether the book my father would finally have produced. I am sure he would have brought his statistics up to date and taken account of new data. Moreover, his thought was changing toward the end. He was growing far more acutely conscious of the necessity for devoting energy and resources to the solving of short-term problems, noting that we can hardly face the problems of the next millenium if we cannot make it through the next century. But there seem to be no surviving articulations of such thoughts. I am also certain my father expected to write a great deal more about Survivalist tactics. His outlines called for discussing "Lessons of Past Social Movements: Early Christianity, Anticlericalism, Abolitionism, the Labor Movement, the Anticolonial Movement, the Women's Movement, etc." as well as the histories of "Conservationism, the Ecology Movement, the Peace Movement, Science Activism (Pugwash, FAS, etc.), the Youth Movement, UNEP, Club of Rome, etc." He expected to discuss the importance to Survivalists of the ideals of science and truth: "Implying heavy reliance on such methods as dedication, discipline, emulation of models, sense of mission, etc." None of these things were spelled out in the materials I have, and I felt no wish to put words into my father's mouth.

As to what I have, and what I used, I list below the major sources for each of the chapters:

Preface Dedicatory: Various typescript drafts.

Chapter 1: Various typescript drafts.

Chapter 2: Various typescript drafts with holograph corrections.

Chapter 3: "The Coming Age of Shortages," *Bulletin of Atomic Scientists* 32 (January 1976): 6–16; "A Dynamic Equilibrium Economy," *Bulletin of Atomic Scientists* 32 (February 1976): 47–55.

Chapter 4: "A Dynamic Equilibrium Economy"; "First Steps to Survival," *Bulletin of Atomic Scientists* 32 (March 1976): 41–48; an untitled typescript fragment; "The Inflation-Unemployment Tradeoff and Full Economic Recovery," *American Journal of Economics and Sociology* 34 (October 1975): 338–44; "Full Employment Policy Revisited," *New Republic* 168 (April 28, 1973): 22; "Development through Restraints on Material Growth," *Focus* 25 (November-December 1974): 11–16; "International Inequality: Is It Really an Important Issue?" (Published symposium paper delivered at the meeting of the International Political Science Association, University of Louvain, September 1971); "World Hunger: Three Approaches" (Unpublished symposium paper delivered at the Conference on World Hunger given by the Cathedral Church of Saint John the Divine and the Graymoor Ecumenical Institute, New York, November 19, 1975); the author's typescript prospectus for this book; "A Survivalist Manifesto" (Symposium paper presented to the IX International Congress of Anthropological and Ethnological Sciences, Chicago, 1973), published in *Social Policy* 4 (November-December 1973): 17; "Growth, Survival and the Market" (Symposium paper delivered at the American Association for the Advancement of Science meeting, Denver, February 21, 1977).

Chapter 5: "First Steps To Survival"; "Psychological Elements in the Survival Crisis," typescript fragment; unpublished symposium piece on "The Greed for Power and Human Survival";

unpublished seninar paper on "The Fear of Death and Human
Survival"; untitled manuscript fragment; "Must Growth
Stop?" *Columbia Journal of World Business* 7 (May-June 1972): 41.
Postscript: "The Fear of Death and Human Survival."

I have also drawn to a lesser degree on other sources.

What I have put together gives, I hope, some hint of the
magisterial scope of my father's mind, of his brilliance in
seeing relationships between the ostensibly unrelated, of his
conscience and his passion. But more than that, it is my
earnest wish that the book be read, attended to, and treated
as a guide in the dark years my father foresaw lying ahead.

I would like to thank my stepmother, Mrs. Etta Benoit,
and Professor Kenneth Boulding of the University of Colorado at Boulder for the help and advice they gave me in the
editing of this book.

ABOUT THE AUTHOR
AND EDITOR

E MILE BENOIT was from 1974 until his death in 1978 a Senior Research Associate and Professor Emeritus of the Graduate School of Business of Columbia University.

Dr. Benoit was the author of *Defense and Economic Growth in Developing Countries* (1973) and *Europe at Sixes and Sevens* (1961), and editor of *Disarmament and World Economic Independence* (1966) and *Disarmament and the Economy* (1962). He was also a contributor to *The Liberal Papers, The Crossroads Papers, Economics and the Idea of Mankind, Role Theory,* and *Southeast Asia's Economy in the 1970s,* and the author of over a hundred contributions to symposia and learned and popular journals in the fields of economics, international relations, international business, philosophy, sociology, and environmental problems.

Dr. Benoit was educated at Harvard (B.A., M.A., Ph.D.) and spent ten years in government service, five of them in the American Embassies in London and Vienna, before coming to Columbia in 1956. He served as consultant to the United Nations, the U.S. Departments of State and Defense, and the Asian Development Bank.

*J*ACK BENOIT GOHN is presently a student at the University of Maryland School of Law. Dr. Gohn is the compiler of *Kingsley Amis: A Checklist (1976)*, and has published articles on literature and law in *Saturday Review*, *Pennsylvania Gazette, Notes and Queries, The Keats-Shelley Journal, The Wordsworth Circle*, and *The Maryland Law Review*. He is a regular contributor to the Baltimore *Sunday Sun*.

Dr. Gohn holds a B.A. and M.A. from the University of Pennsylvania and an M.A. and Ph.D. from the John Hopkins University.